Deported to the wrong country: Impact of Trump's deportations

Also by DM Ole Kiminta

How the Western Democracies failed the world (KBros)
Supporting Refugees in their Homelands (Kbros)
Dissuading Global War Mongers (KBros)
Dissuading war mongers (KBros)
La Libération Monétaire en Afrique (KBros)
Canada Post: Management failure to modernise mail systems
Live to be 200 (KBros)
Aim to live to be 200 (KBros)
Western democracies failed the world economies (KBros)
Wrong foot forward: US-Canada trade wars (KBros)
Canada begs to differ: Never a 51st state of USA (KBros)
Tethered to the Kitchen (KBros)
Nous ne pouvons pas être le 51e État des États-Unis (KBros)
Nous ne serons jamais le 51ème état des États-Unis. (KBros)
The Nephilim and the erosion of moral boundaries (KBros)
Every human is an advocate for World Peace (KBros)
The diplomatic dilemma of Western Sahara (KBros)
Every human: Advocate for World Peace (KBros)
The last blue planet (KBros)
Europeans divided & shaped Arab World (KBros)
Thuggery: What led to October 7th incident? (Kbros)
Breaking Free: Abandoning dependency on foreign currencies in Africa (Kindle Edition)
When white people were slaves: White Slavery (Kindle Edition)
Les consequences des colons francais sur Amazighs marocains: Contexte historique de la colonisation francais au Maroc (French Edition) Kindle Edition
L'Écoute qui Transforme: Renforcer la Confiance des Enfants à l'École: L'importance de la communication

enfants-enseignants en classe (French Edition) Kindle Edition

Mastering Emotions: How to avoid Anger and jealousy: Anger and jealousy are destructive *(Kindle Edition)*

Maasai initiation in today's society *(Kindle edition)*

Hidden dangers of fully integrated AI world: Quality education with AI for future generation *(Kindle edition)*

One Africa: The premise & perils of political integration *(Kindle)*

Early foreign visitors into African nations: Fortune seekers *(Kindle)*

Deported to the wrong country: Impact of Trump's deportations

Deported to the wrong country: Impact of Trump's deportations

Printed in Canada

Book and cover design: (© KBros)

Written by: DM Ole Kiminta

ISBN - Paperback: 9781069498670

Table of contents

Chapter 1: Overview of deportation trends

The landscape of deportation trends has evolved significantly over the past few decades, particularly concerning non-African immigrants from Western countries. Being arrested and right away being deported to pre-arranged prisons in some African countries. Data reveal a sharp increase in deportations, driven by stringent immigration policies and national security concerns. Countries such as the United States, the United Kingdom, and various EU nations have implemented aggressive deportation practices, often targeting specific nationalities and demographics. This trend raises pressing questions about the implications of these policies on individuals and the societies to which they are returned.

Legal challenges faced by deported non-African immigrants to African prison camps are a crucial aspect of this discussion. Many deportees encounter complex legal hurdles that hinder their ability to contest their deportation. The legal frameworks surrounding immigration and deportation are often opaque, with limited access to legal representation for those affected one reason being that the deportees may have violated visa stay period or committed crimes and are deported within hours after being arrested hence, there is no time to seek legal representations. This lack of support can exacerbate the trauma associated with deportation, leaving individuals feeling powerless and isolated in unfamiliar environments.

For the mental health of non-African immigrants who find themselves being arrested and shipped out, studies indicate that many individuals experience heightened levels of anxiety, depression, and post-traumatic stress disorder following their deportation. The abrupt separation from established communities and support networks can lead to feelings of abandonment and rejection. Such mental health challenges are compounded by the social stigma that often accompanies deportation, making reintegration into society even more difficult.

Social acceptance of deported non-African immigrants varies widely across different African countries. While some communities may easily go along with their government accepting foreign deportees into their countries and therefore loathe the idea of hostility towards them, others may view them with suspicion or hostility. This social stigma can significantly affect the process, as deportees often struggle to find employment (if allowed) and rebuild their lives. Furthermore, the role of diaspora networks becomes vital in facilitating the reintegration journey, providing support and resources to help individuals navigate their new realities, that is if at all they will be granted parole and be allowed to stay in the African countries after their prison time, however, we have no idea what the end game is with these new arrangements or agreements among Africa-Europe and the American governments agreements.

Comparative analyses of deportation policies across Western countries reveal a patchwork of approaches, each with its unique implications for deported individuals. At this juncture, no information is available of whether these deported individuals being sent to countries that is not their origin are regarded (criminals, deportees, etc.). Countries differ not only in the number of deportations but also in their treatment of foreign deportees upon arrival to the countries hosting the deportees. Non-governmental organisations play a pivotal role in supporting deported non-African immigrants, offering resources and advocacy to address their needs. As these trends continue to unfold, understanding the complexities surrounding the arrests and deportations in Europeans countries and United States and shipping them to African countries is essential for fostering a more humane approach to immigration policy.

Historical context of non-African deportation to African countries

The historical context of deportation of immigrants reveals a complex interplay of socio-political factors that have shaped the treatment of immigrants in Western countries. Over the decades, waves of migration brought diverse groups to Europe and North America, each seeking better opportunities but often facing backlash from segments of society. This backdrop of immigration has been influenced by economic conditions, political climates, and global events, leading to varying degrees of acceptance and hostility towards the immigrants. As economic pressures mount and nationalist sentiments rise, deportation has emerged as a tool for governments to manage perceived threats to social cohesion and national identity.

Deportation policies in Western nations have evolved significantly, reflecting changing political ideologies and legal frameworks. In the post-World War II era, many countries adopted more lenient approaches, focusing on integration and support for refugees and immigrants. However, as the 21st century unfolded, a shift towards stricter immigration controls became evident, with increased surveillance and enforcement measures. This transition has resulted in the systematic deportation of many immigrants, often justified by claims of illegal residency or criminal behaviour, regardless of the immigrants' contributions to society.

The human rights implications of these deportation policies are profound, raising ethical questions about the treatment of individuals who often have deep ties to their host countries. Deportees frequently face legal challenges that complicate their return to their countries of origin, where they may encounter further difficulties, including stigma and lack of support. The psychological impact of deportation also cannot be understated; many individuals experience trauma, anxiety, and depression as they grapple with the loss of their homes and communities, leading to long-term mental health issues.

Moreover, social stigma surrounding deported individuals can hinder their reintegration into society. Many deportees struggle to find acceptance in their new home communities, which may view them through a lens of shame or failure. This stigma can exacerbate feelings of isolation and hopelessness, making it difficult for them to rebuild their lives. The role of NGOs in supporting these individuals is crucial, providing essential resources and advocacy to help them navigate the complexities of reintegration and overcome the barriers they face.

In conclusion, understanding the historical context of non-African deportees being deported to African prison camps is vital for addressing the ongoing challenges faced by deported individuals. By examining case studies of specific nationalities and the comparative analysis of deportation policies across Western countries, we can better appreciate the nuances of this issue. The influence of diaspora networks and cultural adjustment experiences further highlight the need for a compassionate approach to deportation, one that acknowledges the humanity of those affected and strives for their successful reintegration into society although we are witnessing the opposite of this at the present time.

Purpose and Scope of the Book

This book, "Deported to wrong countries": The Journey of Non-African Deportees to Africa," aims to shed light on the complex and often misunderstood experiences of non-African immigrants who find themselves deported from Western countries to Africa. In recent years, there has been a significant increase in the number of deportees, many of whom face numerous challenges as they navigate their return to a continent that may feel foreign to them. By exploring these experiences, the book seeks to provide a comprehensive understanding of the multifaceted issues surrounding deportation and reintegration.

The purpose of this book therefore, extends beyond merely documenting the journeys of these deportees; it aims to highlight the legal challenges they encounter upon their return. Many deported individuals face a labyrinth of legal hurdles that complicate their reintegration into society. This includes issues related to residency status, access to social services, and legal representation, which can further exacerbate their already precarious situations. Through detailed case studies, the book will illustrate the specific challenges faced by various nationalities, offering a nuanced perspective on the immigration policies of Western nations.

We are aware that during the two world wars, prisoners of war were being shipped to work in foreign countries that were under colonial or occupation by European countries just because those countries had no say to reject these practices by the colonisers. There were prisoners of war (POW) from Italy, Japan, and more who were in Gilgil town and other countryside in Kenya doing hard labour and much more until towards the end of the war. In today's narrative, it is the African countries such as Uganda, Rwanda, Angola etc who are willingly accepting foreign deportees from elsewhere under an agreement with American and European countries especially Britain, France, Germany, etc to host the deportees.

For the deportees, mental health is another critical aspect addressed in this book. The trauma of deportation can have lasting effects on the mental well-being of individuals, often leading to feelings of isolation, anxiety, and depression. By examining the psychological impact of deportation, the book aims to raise awareness about the need for mental health support services tailored to the needs of deported non-African immigrants. This exploration will also consider the role of social stigma and community acceptance in shaping the experiences of these individuals as they attempt to reintegrate into their new environments.

Furthermore, the book delves into the human rights implications of deportation policies implemented by Western countries. It questions the ethical considerations of such policies and their impact on the lives of deportees. By analysing the role of non-governmental organisations (NGOs) that assist deported immigrants in Africa, the book will provide insights into the support systems available to these individuals. The involvement of diaspora networks will also be examined, as these connections can significantly influence the reintegration process and cultural adjustment experiences.

I would like to mention to the reader that there are African families that are caught in this haphazard dragnet of "Arrest and deport at once" and paradoxically, they end up being deported to Africa but to the wrong African country, for example, an Algerian family being shipped to Uganda or Rwanda or Angola instead of being deported back to Algeria.

Ultimately, "Deported to wrong country" aims to foster a deeper understanding of the complexities surrounding deportation and the broader implications for society. It invites readers to engage with the stories of deported non-African immigrants and consider the systemic changes necessary to improve their circumstances. This exploration is not just about the individuals affected but also about the societal responsibility to address the issues of migration, legality, and human rights in an increasingly interconnected world.

One might wonder why some countries decided to deport some individuals and ship them out, it depends on the country, in Europe, it has become very difficult to control the flow of illegal migrants while in USA, the government has a mandate to deport as many as possible to any country that will take them and hence, this is the picture we are dealing with right now (2025).

More than 2,200 lives have been lost since June, the UN refugee agency UNHCR believes.

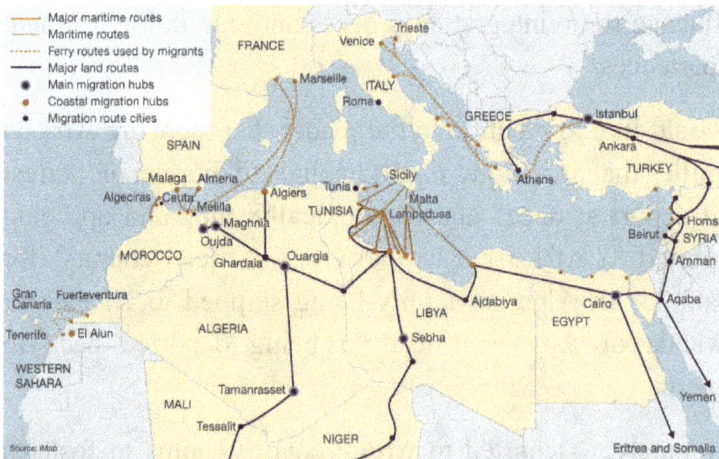

The above shows routes used by many individuals trying to get to Europe.

We can only attribute the increased numbers of the dead to the additional individuals attempting to reach Europe. That is because of the big increase in numbers crossing the Mediterranean. While some 60,000 reached European shores in 2013, so far more than 130,000 have arrived in 2014 and more increase as years go by.

While many of them are trying to get across to the Iberian Peninsula, the majority of migrants head for Italy, prompting a crisis that the country's navy, coast guard and beleaguered immigration facilities are struggling to handle because of the huge number of them coming in.

In spite of so many dying, they keep coming, for instant, in October of 2013, 366 people died off the Italian island of Lampedusa when the fishing boat they were travelling in from Libya capsized. Only a fraction of these people can swim and they themselves know the dangers on these waters, yet they keep coming expecting to be rescued.

Around or up to 2014, almost all the victims were from Eritrea according to UNHCR. Migrants crossing in the central Mediterranean - from Libya and Tunisia - have until recently come mostly from Eritrea and Somalia, although increasing numbers of Syrians fleeing the country's civil war are also were making the journey.

On the African shore, Libya has been, and has become a popular starting point for many journeys, with people traffickers taking advantage of the country's power vacuum and increasing lawlessness which set in after Qadafi's exit.

The distance across is short and hence relatively short to Lampedusa encourages more people to risk the journey crossing over while unaware of dangerous winds and unreliable dinghies that they use to transport them.

The groups of charities that aid the people crossing the waters believe that more than 20,000 people may have died at sea trying to reach Europe in the last two decades and it seems to increase each year.

To say the least, the waters of mediterranean is filled with perished people and in most cases, children and older people who cannot swim and some of us wonders how the refugees with minimal education, no skills, language problems can contribute to other developed countries and so, the solution, in my opinion, is try to help and support the refugees in their own country by taking the issues with the governments of where they come from (If it is possible) because some of them have no political persecution or any civil unrest or any kind of war problem in their home lands, they just decide to pack-up and head for Europe. These are the ones that can be helped in their own countries depending on co-operation of their governments to allow this kind of external support.

Migration in the Mediterranean
Numbers of 'irregular migrants' detected

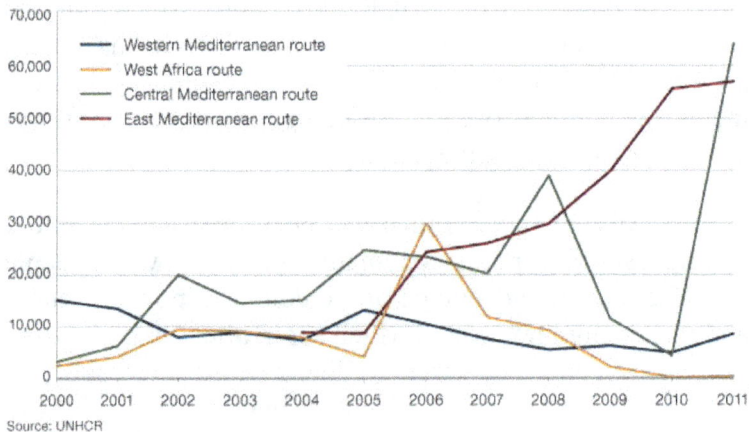

Source: UNHCR

source: UNHCR

At the end of the first quarter of 2022, more than 18,000 refugees and migrants crossed the Mediterranean to reach Europe, majority of them aiming for Britain, France, Germany and Italy. Altogether, more than 2.3 million have taken this same journey in the past eight years according to available data.

In 2014, more than 200,000 refugees and migrants moved from East and West Africa to North Africa and onwards to Europe's shores. The scale of movement peaked in 2015, with over 1 million refugees and migrants arriving in Europe, all looking for a better life and nothing substantial to offer or give back, this is why the citizens of the countries feel short-changed and advocate for the refugees removal.

Within two years in 2016, the number of individuals arriving to Europe dropped below 400,000 and continued to gradually decrease in the following years, hitting a low at the beginning of the COVID-19 pandemic in 2020.

During the Covid peak years, most countries had locked their borders and hence, low arrivals during the pandemic are likely associated with measures to prevent the spread of the corona virus crisis on global remittances from diaspora communities.

With all the precautions and measures implemented in 2020, the human smugglers found other ways quickly and adapted to offer alternative ways of bypassing official controls and since 2021, refugee or illegal migrant numbers have once again started to increase, with figures suggesting an upward trend regardless of enforcements.

So far, between 2014 and 2021, more than 24,400 lives have been lost or are said to be missing while trying to cross the Mediterranean Sea while others have suffered unspeakable violations of their human rights.

It is true that some of those crossing the Mediterranean are searching for a better life and economic opportunities, many are seeking safety from conflict, violence or persecution. Looking at the data of the most common countries of origin for people moving along Mediterranean routes, we notice that those affected by years of conflict and displacement, where human rights abuses are not uncommon, and some of the largest refugee and internal displacement crises due to conflict are in the East and Horn of Africa, that is Somali, Eritrea, Ethiopia, and some from Yemen and Zanzibar. The rest come from North African and West African countries. During the year 2021, Ethiopia features among the top 10 internal displacement crises worldwide, while Eritrea is among the top 10 refugee crises and Somalia, South Sudan and Sudan appear among the top 10 for both types of crises and also this same region has many individuals making their way illegally to USA and Canada through the Caribbean, south America and Mexico

Chapter 2: Legal challenges faced by deportees

Understanding Deportation Laws in Western Countries

Deportation laws in Western countries are complex and often vary significantly from one nation to another. Understanding these laws is crucial for non-African immigrants facing the risk of deportation. The legal frameworks typically involve various factors such as immigration status, criminal history, and the country of origin. Each country has its own specific processes and criteria that determine who can be deported and under what circumstances, leading to a myriad of legal challenges for those affected. The consequences of these laws extend beyond mere expulsion, impacting individuals' lives profoundly.

The legal challenges faced by deported non-African immigrants upon being shipped to Africa can be daunting. Many find themselves grappling with bureaucratic hurdles, including issues related to citizenship, residency, and access to basic services. The lack of support and resources often exacerbates their situation, making it difficult to integrate into their new home communities. Furthermore, the legal systems in some African countries may not provide adequate protections for new deportees, leaving them vulnerable to exploitation and discrimination.

Many deportees experience feelings of shame, isolation, and trauma as they navigate the challenges of being shipped to a place they may not have lived before or if they get lucky to be shipped to their original countries, they may not have lived there for years or those with children born overseas now trying to settle and grapple a foreign culture. The stigma associated with being deported can lead to social exclusion, further exacerbating mental health issues. Support systems are often lacking, and the lack of understanding from local communities can contribute to a sense of hopelessness among deportees.

Social stigma and community acceptance play a significant role in the integration process of deported non-African immigrants. Some communities may view deportees with suspicion or disdain, which can hinder their ability to rebuild their lives. This societal rejection often forces deportees into isolation, limiting their opportunities for employment and social engagement. Understanding the dynamics of community acceptance is essential for developing programmes that facilitate smoother integration and promote social harmony.

Human rights implications of deportation policies in Western countries are also critical to consider. Many argue that these policies disproportionately affect vulnerable populations and violate fundamental human rights. Case studies of specific nationalities among deported non-African immigrants reveal patterns of discrimination and systemic inequities that need addressing. Although support for these individuals do not exist in some countries, the role of NGOs in supporting deported immigrants in African countries is vital, as they provide essential resources and advocacy to help individuals navigate their challenges and foster better reintegration into society.

Legal rights of deportees in Africa

Deportation processes across Africa raise significant legal questions regarding the rights of deportees, particularly those from non-African countries. In many instances, deported individuals find themselves in a legal limbo, grappling with the lack of clear guidelines and support systems that should protect their rights. The challenge lies in the fact that many African nations do not have comprehensive legal frameworks specifically addressing the rights of deportees. This inadequacy often leads to violations of basic human rights, as deportees may be denied access to legal representation or essential services such as healthcare and housing upon their arrival.

The legal challenges faced by African deportees and non-African deportees in African countries can be exacerbated by the stigma attached to deportation. Many deportees experience social ostracism, which can severely affect their ability to reintegrate into local communities. This social stigma often manifests in discrimination in employment opportunities and social interactions, further complicating their legal status and access to justice. Additionally, the psychological impact of deportation can lead to mental health issues, creating a vicious cycle of marginalisation and exclusion.

Human rights implications surrounding deportation policies implemented by Western countries also play a crucial role in shaping the experiences of deported non-African immigrants. Many of these policies are viewed as punitive rather than rehabilitative, leaving individuals without the necessary support to adapt to their new environment. The implications extend beyond the immediate effects on deportees; they also challenge the legal obligations of African states under international human rights laws, raising questions about their commitment to protect the rights of all individuals within their borders.

NGOs operate as vital support systems for deported individuals, providing legal assistance, mental health resources, and reintegration programmes. These organisations often bridge the gap between deportees and local communities, advocating for their rights and facilitating their adjustment to life in Africa. The efforts of NGOs can significantly alleviate the burdens faced by deportees, allowing them to rebuild their lives and reintegrate more effectively into society.

In summary, the legal rights of deportees in Africa are complex and often inadequately addressed. The intersection of social stigma, mental health challenges, and the role of NGOs highlights the multifaceted nature of deportation experiences. Understanding these elements is crucial for developing more humane policies that respect the rights and dignity of deported individuals as they navigate their shipment to African country.

Obstacles to legal recourse

The journey of non-African deportees to Africa is fraught with numerous obstacles, particularly when it comes to legal recourse. Many deportees find themselves caught in a complex web of immigration laws that are often unfavourable and difficult to navigate. The lack of familiarity with local legal systems, coupled with language barriers and insufficient legal representation, makes it challenging for deportees to assert their rights or contest their deportation effectively. These hurdles can lead to a sense of helplessness and frustration, as individuals grapple with the stark reality of their situation without adequate support.

Another significant obstacle arises from the limited understanding of human rights implications surrounding deportation policies in Western countries. Many deportees are unaware of the legal protections available to them or the grounds on which they might challenge their deportation orders. This lack of knowledge is further compounded by the social stigma that often accompanies deportation, which can discourage individuals from seeking legal help or asserting their rights. As a result, many remain silent victims of a system that seems to marginalise their experiences and concerns.

The psychological toll of being forcibly removed from a familiar environment and thrust into a new and often unwelcoming society can lead to severe emotional distress. Deportees may experience anxiety, depression, and feelings of isolation as they navigate their new reality. These mental health challenges are exacerbated by the aforementioned legal obstacles, creating a vicious cycle that hinders recovery and reintegration into society.

Community acceptance plays a pivotal role in the reintegration process for deported African and non-African immigrants. However, social stigma often leads to marginalisation, making it difficult for deportees to find support within their new or former communities. The perception of deportees as criminals or failures can prevent them from accessing essential services, including legal assistance and mental health support. This societal rejection can further entrench them in a state of despair, complicating their efforts to rebuild their lives in African country where they eventually end up.

Supporting deported non-African immigrants is crucial in addressing these obstacles. The organisations such as NGO's often provide legal aid, counselling services, and community integration programmes that empower deportees to reclaim their lives. By facilitating access to resources and fostering community acceptance, NGOs can help mitigate the adverse effects of deportation and promote a more inclusive environment for non-African immigrants. Their work highlights the importance of solidarity and support in overcoming the multifaceted challenges faced by deportees.

Chapter 3: Psychological effects of deportation

The psychological effects of deportation on non-African immigrants are profound, often leading to a range of mental health challenges. Many deportees experience feelings of loss, anxiety, and depression as they grapple with the abrupt end of their dreams and aspirations in their host countries. This sudden transition can create a sense of hopelessness, particularly when individuals are sent back to environments that may not be welcoming or familiar. The trauma associated with being forcibly removed from one's home, even if it was a temporary residence, can leave lasting scars on mental well-being.

Social stigma plays a critical role in shaping the experiences of deported individuals. Upon their being shipped to Africa, some that have returned to their original countries face judgement and prejudice from their communities, which can exacerbate feelings of isolation and rejection. This stigma often stems from misconceptions about the circumstances surrounding their deportation and the belief that they have failed in their endeavours abroad. As a result, reintegration becomes not just a physical challenge but also an emotional one, as deportees work to rebuild their identities in societies that may view them unfavourably.

Legal challenges compound the difficulties faced by deportees, adding an additional layer of stress to an already challenging situation. Many non-African deportees may find themselves navigating complex legal systems that are not designed to support their reintegration. The lack of legal assistance and advocacy can leave them vulnerable to exploitation and further marginalisation. This systemic failure to provide necessary legal support often impacts their mental health, as the uncertainty regarding their status and rights can lead to increased anxiety and despair.

Finally, the influence of diaspora networks emerges as a significant factor in the reintegration of deported individuals. These networks can offer emotional support, resources, and a sense of community that are crucial for overcoming the challenges of returning to a home country. The connections forged through these networks can alleviate feelings of isolation and provide a pathway to rebuilding lives. As deportees navigate their new reality, the support from diaspora communities can be a beacon of hope, aiding in their recovery and adjustment to life after deportation.

The existing healthcare infrastructure in many African countries is often underfunded and lacks the necessary resources to adequately support mental health needs. This situation is further complicated by the stigma surrounding mental health, which can deter individuals from seeking the help they require. Consequently, many deportees find themselves without necessary support systems during their reintegration process.

Many deportees may not be aware of their rights or the available resources due to language barriers or a lack of information. Additionally, the legal status of deportees can render them hesitant to seek help, fearing potential repercussions or further marginalisation. This creates a cycle where untreated mental health issues can exacerbate legal and social challenges, impacting the overall wellbeing of individuals trying to rebuild their lives in a new environment.

There are many deportees who experience feelings of rejection, isolation, and anxiety, which can lead to severe mental health conditions such as depression or PTSD. Without adequate access to mental health services, these individuals may struggle to cope with their feelings, leading to further social alienation. Community acceptance is essential for recovery; however, social stigma often prevents deportees from integrating into their new communities, perpetuating their mental health struggles.

In conclusion, the interplay of access to mental health services, legal challenges, and social stigma creates a complex landscape for non-African deportees in Africa. Addressing these issues requires a multi-faceted approach that includes improving healthcare infrastructure, providing legal support, and fostering community acceptance. By understanding the unique challenges faced by deportees, stakeholders can work towards creating a more supportive environment that prioritises mental health and wellbeing, ultimately aiding in successful reintegration into society.

Case studies on mental health outcomes

Case studies on mental health outcomes for non-African deportees reveal a complex interplay of factors that significantly impact their well-being. Many deportees experience heightened levels of anxiety and depression upon their return to Africa, often exacerbated by the abrupt transition from their host countries. For instance, a study focusing on Somali deportees from the UK highlighted that the isolation and lack of support systems in their home country led to an increased prevalence of mental health issues. These findings underscore the importance of understanding the unique challenges faced by deportees as they navigate their reintegration into society.

Another key aspect of mental health outcomes relates to social stigma and community acceptance. Deportees frequently encounter prejudices that can hinder their ability to reintegrate effectively. In a case study involving deported individuals from the United States to Nigeria, many reported feelings of shame and rejection from their communities. This social stigma not only affects their mental health but also their ability to find employment and rebuild their lives. Addressing these perceptions is crucial for fostering a more supportive environment for returning migrants.

Various organisations have initiated programmes aimed at providing psychological support and facilitating community acceptance for deportees. For example, in South Africa, NGOs have developed counselling services tailored to the needs of deportees from different nationalities. These initiatives not only offer mental health resources but also encourage community dialogue to reduce stigma, demonstrating the potential for positive change through targeted support efforts.

Comparative analyses of deportation policies across Western countries reveal differing impacts on mental health outcomes. Countries with more comprehensive reintegration programmes tend to see better mental health results among deportees. For instance, deportees from Canada to various African nations often benefit from pre-departure counselling and post-arrival support, which contrasts sharply with the experiences of those deported from other Western nations lacking such initiatives. This highlights the critical need for policymakers to consider the mental health implications of their deportation policies.

In summary, examining case studies of non-African deportees illuminates the intricate relationship between deportation, mental health, and community dynamics. The findings suggest that without adequate support systems, deportees are at a greater risk for mental health issues, compounded by social stigma. Furthermore, the involvement of NGOs and favourable policy frameworks can significantly enhance the reintegration experience, promoting better mental health outcomes for these individuals as they attempt to rebuild their lives in a challenging environment.

Chapter 4: Social Stigma and Community Acceptance

Perceptions of Deportees in host communities

The perceptions of deportees in host communities play a critical role in shaping their reintegration experiences. Many non-African deportees from Western countries encounter a complex social landscape upon their return to Africa. Often, these individuals are viewed through a lens of stigma which can profoundly impact their ability to reclaim their identities and establish a sense of belonging. The narratives surrounding deportees are frequently marred by misconceptions, leading to prejudices that hinder their acceptance within local populations.

Social stigma is not merely a personal burden; it has broader implications for community dynamics. Host communities may perceive deportees as failures who could not navigate the systems of their host countries, leading to a reluctance to engage with them. This perception can result in isolation, as deportees might be shunned or treated with suspicion by locals. Moreover, the lack of understanding regarding the circumstances of deportation can exacerbate these negative feelings, further alienating returning individuals from their communities.

The mental health of non-African deportees is often adversely affected by the perceptions they face in their host communities. The stress of reintegration, compounded by social rejection, can lead to feelings of depression, anxiety, and low self-worth. Many deportees grapple with the dual challenge of adjusting to a home they may not fully recognise while simultaneously battling the negative perceptions held by others. Addressing mental health needs is therefore crucial, as it not only affects the deportee's well-being but also their ability to reintegrate successfully.

Organisations that work with deportees play a vital role in mitigating these challenges. NGOs often provide essential support services, including counselling and community engagement initiatives designed to foster understanding and acceptance. These organisations aim to bridge the gap between deportees and host communities, promoting narratives that highlight the shared humanity of all individuals, regardless of their past. By tackling social stigma head-on, these initiatives can help reshape perceptions and pave the way for more inclusive communities.

The role of diaspora networks can offer crucial support and resources that assist deportees in navigating their new realities. By fostering connections with supportive individuals and groups, deportees can combat isolation and stigma, ultimately enhancing their chances of successful reintegration. Understanding the nuanced perceptions of deportees in host communities is essential for addressing the broader implications of deportation policies and their impacts on human rights and social justice.

Factors influencing community acceptance

Community acceptance of deported non-African immigrants is influenced by a myriad of factors, each playing a crucial role in shaping the experiences of these individuals upon their return to Africa. One of the primary elements is the cultural perception of deportees within the host communities. Many local residents may hold negative stereotypes or preconceived notions about deported individuals, often viewing them as failures or undesirables. Such perceptions can lead to social ostracism, making it challenging for returnees to reintegrate and establish a sense of belonging in their communities.

Another significant factor is the socio-economic status of the deportees and the communities to which they return. Often, deportees arrive with limited resources and skills that can hinder their ability to contribute economically. If the local community is struggling with its own economic challenges, there may be less willingness to accept newcomers. This economic strain can exacerbate tensions between deportees and local residents, as competition for jobs and resources increases.

Furthermore, the role of local governance and policies in addressing the needs of deported individuals should be amplified. That is, communities with supportive local leadership and policies aimed at facilitating integration can foster a more welcoming environment for returnees. In contrast, areas lacking such support may see heightened resistance to accepting deportees, further complicating their reintegration process.

Social networks, including family ties and friendships, also significantly affect community acceptance. Deportees who can leverage existing relationships may find it easier to navigate the challenges of reintegration. These networks often provide emotional support and practical assistance, enabling a smoother transition back into society. Conversely, those without strong connections may struggle more profoundly, facing isolation and alienation from their peers.

Finally, the media portrayal of deported immigrants plays a role in shaping public perception and acceptance. Negative or sensationalised coverage can reinforce biases and fears within the community, while positive stories highlighting successful reintegration can help mitigate stigma. Therefore, fostering a balanced narrative around deported individuals is essential for promoting acceptance and understanding within the broader community.

Strategies for Overcoming Stigma

Stigma often follows deported non-African immigrants as they attempt to reintegrate into their communities in Africa. Overcoming this stigma requires a multifaceted approach that addresses both personal and societal perceptions. Firstly, education plays a pivotal role in changing attitudes. By informing the public about the circumstances that lead to deportation, misconceptions can be dispelled. Awareness campaigns highlighting the contributions deportees can make to society can also foster a more accepting environment.

Building support networks within the community is another essential strategy. These networks can provide a sense of belonging and facilitate connections with others who have faced similar challenges. Community organisations and NGOs can play a crucial role in creating safe spaces for deportees to share their experiences and receive support. This not only helps individuals cope with their situation but also encourages community members to engage and empathise with their stories.

Engaging in dialogue with local leaders and influencers can further aid in combating stigma. By involving respected community figures in discussions about the realities of deportation, a broader understanding can be cultivated. Workshops and forums led by these leaders can help shift narratives and promote inclusiveness. This grassroots approach encourages community ownership of the reintegration process, making it more likely that stigma will be reduced.

Mental health support is a vital component in overcoming stigma. Many deportees experience trauma and mental health challenges as a result of their experiences. Providing access to counselling and mental health services can help individuals heal and rebuild their lives. When deportees are supported in their mental well-being, they are better equipped to face societal challenges and advocate for their rights.

Lastly, fostering relationships with diaspora networks can significantly aid in overcoming stigma. These networks often offer resources, mentorship, and connections that can ease the transition for deported individuals. By linking deportees with successful members of the diaspora, they can find hope and inspiration, further enabling their reintegration into society. This combined approach of education, community support, dialogue, mental health resources, and diaspora connections can effectively combat the stigma surrounding deported non-African immigrants in Africa.

Chapter 5: Human rights implications of deportation policies

International human rights standards

International human rights standards play a crucial role in shaping the treatment of deported non-African immigrants in Africa. These standards, established by various international treaties and conventions, set the groundwork for the protection of individuals' rights regardless of their nationality or immigration status. They emphasise the importance of dignity, equality, and non-discrimination, which are vital for ensuring that deportees are treated humanely and fairly upon their return to their countries of origin. Understanding these standards is essential for both legal practitioners and the deportees themselves, as they navigate the complexities of their situation in a foreign environment.

The legal challenges faced by deported non-African immigrants often stem from inadequate adherence to these international human rights standards. Many deportees find themselves in precarious situations, lacking access to legal representation or resources to contest their deportation. Furthermore, the lack of transparency in the deportation process raises significant concerns regarding violations of due process. This legal ambiguity can lead to a cycle of vulnerability for deportees, exacerbating their difficulties in reintegrating into their home communities and contributing to further marginalisation.

Social stigma and community acceptance are critical factors in the reintegration journey of deported non-African immigrants. Many individuals face negative perceptions from their peers, which can lead to social exclusion and difficulties in securing employment or housing. This stigma can be rooted in misconceptions about the reasons for deportation, leading to further alienation of these individuals. Efforts to foster community understanding and acceptance of deportees are essential in breaking down these barriers and facilitating their successful reintegration into society.

Case analysis of human rights violations

The analysis of human rights violations related to the deportation of non-African immigrants from Western countries to Africa reveals a complex landscape of legal challenges and societal implications. Many deportees face immediate legal hurdles upon arrival, as they often lack knowledge of local laws and their rights within the new legal framework. This ignorance can lead to further marginalisation, leaving them vulnerable to exploitation and abuse. Understanding the legal landscape is crucial for addressing the injustices faced by these individuals as they navigate their new environments.

Mental health issues are a significant concern for deported non-African immigrants, many of whom experience trauma and distress stemming from their deportation experiences. The abrupt transition to a different cultural and social context can exacerbate feelings of isolation and anxiety. Mental health support services in many African countries are often inadequate, further complicating the reintegration process. Addressing these mental health challenges is essential for fostering a supportive environment for deportees, enabling them to rebuild their lives effectively.

Advocacy for Policy Reform

Advocacy for policy reform is crucial in addressing the myriad challenges faced by non-African deportees returning to Africa. Many of these individuals encounter significant legal hurdles upon their arrival, often landing in a system that is unprepared to deal with their unique circumstances. The advocacy for more humane and supportive policies is essential not only for the individuals but also for the communities that receive them. By working towards reform, advocates can help establish frameworks that protect the rights and dignity of deported immigrants, ensuring that they are not further marginalised upon their return.

One significant aspect of advocacy is raising awareness about the mental health impacts of deportation. Many deported individuals suffer from trauma and stress due to their experiences in Western countries and the abrupt nature of their deportation. By promoting mental health support through policy changes, advocates can help facilitate access to necessary services, enabling deportees to heal and reintegrate into society. This focus on mental health can also reduce the stigma associated with deportation, fostering a more accepting environment within local communities.

Many deportees maintain connections with their communities abroad, which can serve as a powerful resource for reintegration. Advocacy that promotes the establishment and strengthening of these networks can lead to better support systems for deported individuals. By encouraging collaboration between diaspora communities and local stakeholders, advocates can help create a more robust support framework for those returning to Africa.

In conclusion, advocacy for policy reform is essential in addressing the complex challenges faced by non-African deportees. By focusing on legal support, mental health, NGO involvement, and diaspora connections, advocates can push for systemic changes that not only aid deportees but also benefit the communities they return to. Such reforms can foster a more inclusive society, ensuring that deported individuals are treated with the respect and dignity they deserve as they navigate their new reality.

Chapter 6: Case Studies of Specific Nationalities

Deportees from the United States

The phenomenon of deportation from the United States has significantly affected many non-African immigrants who find themselves sent to African countries. These deportees often face a myriad of legal challenges upon arrival, as they grapple with the complexities of immigration laws in their home countries. Many are met with bureaucratic hurdles that complicate their attempts to reintegrate into society. The daunting prospect of navigating these legal systems can often lead to feelings of hopelessness and frustration among deportees, who may have spent years building a life in the United States.

Source: Ricardo IV Tamayo

Mental health repercussions are another critical aspect of the deportation experience. The trauma associated with being forcibly removed from one's home can lead to severe emotional distress, including anxiety and depression. Deportees frequently struggle with the loss of social connections, employment opportunities, and their previous identities. The psychological impact is compounded by the stigma attached to deportation, as many deportees feel ostracised by their communities, which may view them as failures or undeserving of support.

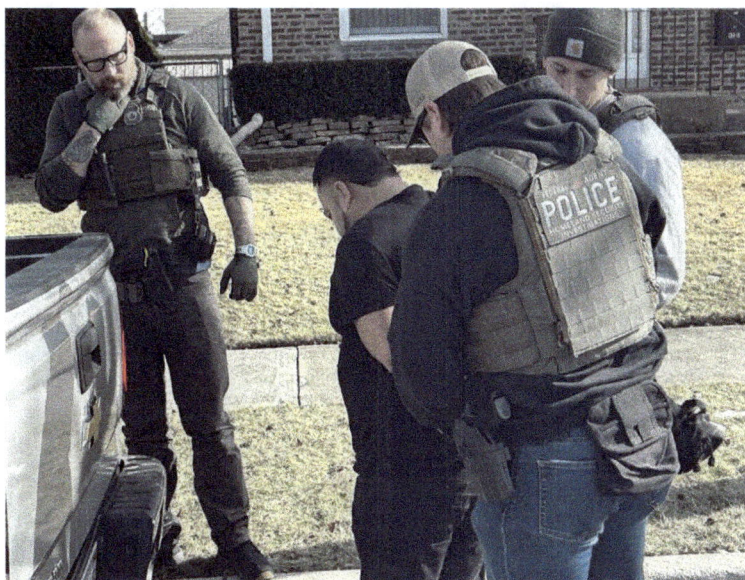

ICE and Department of Homeland Security agents detaining a man

Social acceptance plays a pivotal role in the reintegration process for deported non-African immigrants. Many face significant challenges in being accepted back into their communities due to prevailing negative perceptions surrounding deportation. This social stigma can hinder their ability to find employment and rebuild their lives, forcing some to rely on informal networks for support. Community attitudes towards deportees can vary widely, with some individuals and organisations offering assistance, while others may perpetuate exclusionary practices.

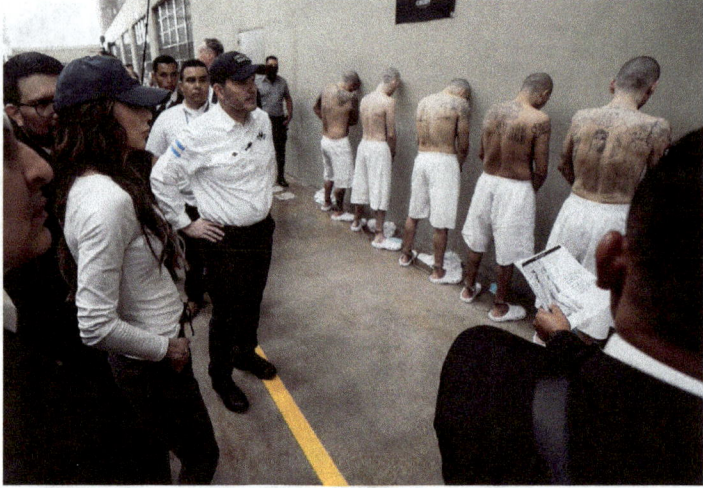

United States Secretary of Homeland Security Kristi Noem touring the
Terrorism Confinement Center in El Salvador on March 26, 2025

Human rights implications of deportation policies in Western countries are increasingly coming under scrutiny. Critics argue that these policies often overlook the humanitarian aspects of deportation, leading to violations of the rights of deportees. Advocacy groups and non-governmental organisations (NGOs) are stepping in to offer support, providing legal aid, mental health resources, and reintegration assistance. These organisations play a crucial role in advocating for the rights of deportees, aiming to create a more supportive environment for their return.

Cultural adjustment experiences also significantly impact deportees as they reintegrate into their home countries. For many, the challenge lies in adapting to a culture they may not have engaged with for years. The influence of diaspora networks often provides a vital lifeline, helping deportees navigate the complexities of return and facilitating their reintegration. Comparative analysis of deportation policies across different Western nations reveals varied approaches and outcomes, showcasing the need for a more humane and understanding framework regarding the treatment of deported individuals.

Deportees from the United Kingdom

The phenomenon of deportation from the United Kingdom has significant implications for non-African immigrants, who often face a myriad of challenges upon being shipped to African countries. These deportees frequently encounter legal hurdles that complicate their reintegration into society. Many find themselves navigating an unfamiliar legal landscape, as the laws of the countries they are deported to may differ drastically from those in the UK. This complexity can lead to prolonged periods of uncertainty, hindering their ability to establish stable lives post-deportation.

Mental health is another critical aspect that merits attention in the context of deportation. Many non-African immigrants experience psychological distress as a result of their forced removal from the UK. The abrupt transition can trigger feelings of isolation, anxiety, and depression, exacerbated by the stigma attached to being deported. As these individuals grapple with their mental health, the lack of adequate support systems in the new home countries can magnify their struggles, making it imperative to address these issues comprehensively.

Social acceptance presents yet another hurdle for deported non-African immigrants. Upon their return, they may face prejudice and discrimination from the communities, who may view them through the lens of their deportation status rather than their individual merits. This social stigma can severely impact their reintegration efforts, as acceptance from new country is often crucial for emotional and social support. Understanding the dynamics of community acceptance is essential for creating effective reintegration programmes that facilitate a smoother transition.

Human rights implications surrounding deportation policies in Western countries are also of paramount importance. Many non-African deportees argue that their rights were violated during the deportation process, leading to calls for a re-examination of these policies. Activists and human rights organisations have raised concerns about the treatment of deportees and the lack of transparency in the deportation process. The focus on human rights is critical in advocating for fair treatment and protection for all immigrants, regardless of their nationality.

Deportees from Canada

The deportation of non-African immigrants from Canada has emerged as a significant issue, drawing attention to the complexities surrounding immigration policies and human rights. Many of those deported are individuals who have lived in Canada for years, often contributing positively to society. Upon their return to Africa, if they are Africans, they face numerous challenges, ranging from legal hurdles to cultural adjustments, significantly impacting their reintegration process. It must be clarified here that unlike other Western countries that are making arrangements with 'any' third country to take deportees, Canada does not do that, they deport people to the countries that the deportees had originated from.

Legal challenges are a prominent concern for deported individuals, as many lack the necessary documentation to navigate the complex legal systems in their home countries. For instance, some may find themselves without access to basic services, employment opportunities, or even housing. The lack of legal recognition can exacerbate feelings of isolation and despair, making it difficult for them to rebuild their lives after deportation.

The mental health implications of deportation cannot be overlooked. Many deportees experience trauma from the abrupt separation from their lives in Canada and the stigma associated with being deported. This psychological toll can lead to issues such as depression and anxiety, hindering their ability to adapt to their new environment. The transition from a familiar setting to an often-unwelcoming community can have lasting effects on their well-being.

Social stigma is another barrier that deported non-African immigrants face upon their return. In many cases, they are viewed with suspicion or disdain by their communities, which can lead to significant social exclusion. Efforts to foster acceptance and understanding within local populations are crucial for aiding the reintegration of these individuals, as societal acceptance plays a vital role in their overall adjustment and mental health.

Despite these challenges, various NGOs are actively working to support deported non-African immigrants as they navigate their new realities

Chapter 7: Role of NGOs in Supporting Deportees

Non-governmental organisations (NGOs) play a pivotal role in addressing the myriad challenges faced by deported non-African immigrants to African countries. Their activities encompass a broad spectrum, from providing immediate humanitarian aid to facilitating long-term reintegration processes. NGOs often step in where governmental support is lacking, ensuring that deportees receive essential services such as shelter, food, and legal assistance. This support is crucial, as many deportees arrive with limited resources and face significant barriers to reintegration into the communities and societies.

One of the primary focuses of NGOs in Africa is the legal challenges that deported individuals encounter. Many deportees struggle to navigate the complex legal landscapes of their host countries, often lacking knowledge of their rights and available resources. NGOs engage in advocacy, helping to educate deportees about their legal standing and providing counsel on how to address potential injustices. This legal assistance is vital not only for individual cases but also for influencing broader policy changes that affect the rights of deportees.

Mental health is another critical area where NGOs have made significant contributions. The trauma associated with deportation can severely impact an individual's psychological well-being.

Social stigma and community acceptance also represent significant challenges for deported non-African immigrants. Many returnees face prejudice and discrimination, which can hinder their ability to rebuild their lives. NGOs work to raise awareness and foster community acceptance through educational programmes and outreach initiatives. By promoting understanding and empathy within local communities, these organisations help create a more supportive environment for deportees, facilitating their reintegration and reducing the social barriers they face.

Lastly, the role of NGOs extends to facilitating connections with diaspora networks, which can be instrumental in helping deportees reintegrate. These networks often provide vital resources, including financial support and employment opportunities. NGOs help bridge the gap between deportees and these networks, promoting collaboration that can enhance the reintegration process. Through these multifaceted efforts, NGOs play an essential role in supporting the journey of non-African deportees as they navigate their new realities in Africa.

Success Stories of NGO Interventions

Non-governmental organisations (NGOs) have played a pivotal role in facilitating the successful reintegration of deported non-African immigrants into their home countries. Through various programmes focused on legal assistance, mental health support, and community acceptance, NGOs have been instrumental in addressing the complex challenges faced by deportees. These interventions have not only provided immediate relief but have also laid the groundwork for long-term stability and acceptance within local communities.

One notable success story is that of an NGO in Nigeria that established a comprehensive support programme for returning deportees from the United States and Europe. By offering legal guidance, vocational training, and mental health counselling, the NGO helped numerous individuals navigate the often-daunting legal landscape upon their return. This initiative not only reduced the stigma associated with deportation but also empowered participants to rebuild their lives and contribute positively to society.

In another instance, an NGO in Ghana focused on the cultural adjustment experiences of deported immigrants. They created community integration workshops that facilitated dialogue between deportees and local residents. These workshops aimed to dismantle preconceived notions about deportees, fostering understanding and acceptance. The positive outcomes included improved relationships and a supportive network for those returning from abroad, showcasing the importance of community involvement in the reintegration process.

Furthermore, NGOs have been crucial in providing mental health support to deportees grappling with the psychological effects of their experiences. Programmes that include counselling and peer support groups have proven effective in helping individuals cope with trauma and social stigma. These mental health initiatives have significantly improved the well-being of many deported immigrants, demonstrating that emotional support is a vital component of successful reintegration.

Many NGOs have collaborated with diaspora organisations to create pathways for deportees to reintegrate effectively. This partnership has facilitated access to resources and opportunities, allowing deported individuals to leverage their connections abroad for better outcomes at home. As a result, these collective efforts highlight the significant impact that targeted NGO interventions can have on the lives of deported non-African immigrants, ultimately promoting human rights and dignity in the face of challenging circumstances.

The collaboration between non-governmental organisations (NGOs) and governments is pivotal in addressing the complex challenges faced by non-African deportees being sent to African countries. These deportees often encounter a myriad of legal obstacles that hinder their reintegration into society. NGOs play a crucial role in bridging the gap between deportees and government services, advocating for the rights of individuals who have been forcibly displaced.

By working together, NGOs and governments can develop comprehensive support systems that enable deportees to navigate the legal landscape more effectively.

One of the significant impacts of deportation is the mental health of the affected individuals. The trauma associated with being deported often leads to psychological distress, which can be exacerbated by a lack of support and understanding from local communities. NGOs are instrumental in providing mental health resources and counselling services tailored to the needs of deportees. By collaborating with government health services, they can ensure that deportees receive the necessary psychological support, facilitating a smoother transition back into their new communities.

Social stigma surrounding deportation can lead to further marginalisation of non-African immigrants. Many deportees face negative perceptions that can affect their ability to reintegrate successfully. NGOs work to combat this stigma by conducting awareness campaigns and fostering community dialogue. Collaborations with governmental bodies can amplify these efforts, promoting policies that encourage acceptance and understanding within local populations, thereby reducing isolation and enhancing community cohesion.

The human rights implications of deportation policies in Western countries is complicated to some degree, NGOs often advocate for the rights of deportees, highlighting cases of unfair treatment and pushing for reforms that protect vulnerable individuals. Through collaboration with governments, these organisations can influence policy changes that better safeguard the rights of deportees, ensuring that their deportation to African country is a dignified process. This partnership is essential for creating a legal framework that respects human rights while addressing the realities of deportation.

Finally, the role of NGOs in supporting deported non-African immigrants extends beyond immediate assistance. They often facilitate cultural adjustment programmes that help deportees acclimatise to their home environments. By working alongside government initiatives, these organisations can create a holistic approach to reintegration that includes language training, job placement services, and community engagement activities. Such collaborations not only aid in the successful reintegration of deportees but also strengthen the capacities of local governments to support their citizens effectively.

Chapter 8: Cultural adjustment experiences

Navigating cultural differences

Navigating cultural differences is a critical aspect for non-African deportees returning to Africa. Many deportees find themselves unprepared for the stark contrasts between Western cultures and the diverse cultures within the African continent. The initial shock often comes from language barriers, differing social norms, and unfamiliar customs. These challenges can lead to feelings of isolation and confusion, making the process of reintegration more complex than anticipated.

For many deportees, cultural adjustment is not merely about adapting to new surroundings; it also involves reconciling their identities shaped by their experiences abroad. They may grapple with a sense of belonging, feeling disconnected from both their home countries elswhere and the countries they were deported from. This internal struggle can exacerbate mental health issues, as they face the dual challenge of cultural adaptation while dealing with the stigma associated with their deportation status.

We must not forget that social stigma plays a significant role in the reintegration process. Many deported individuals encounter prejudice and discrimination from local communities that view them through the lens of their deportation regardless of the situation. This stigma can hinder their ability to find employment, build social networks, and access essential services. As a result, deportees often feel marginalised, which can further complicate their efforts to navigate cultural differences and establish a new life.

Human rights implications surrounding deportation policies in Western countries also intersect with the cultural challenges faced by deportees. Policies that lack consideration for the cultural backgrounds of deportees can lead to further alienation and difficulties in adjusting to life in new country. Advocacy groups and NGOs play a vital role in addressing these concerns by providing resources and support to help deportees navigate their new cultural landscapes and advocate for their rights.

In conclusion, navigating cultural differences is a multifaceted process for non-African deportees sent to African countries. It requires not only individual resilience but also community support and understanding. As these individuals work to rebuild their lives, it is essential for society to foster an inclusive environment that acknowledges their struggles and assists them in their journey towards reintegration. The question of some of these individuals being repatriated to their original countries is not discussed here but it is assumed that unless there is genuine request by a deportee to be sent to their original country, majority of them might have reasons for not asking to be sent to where they had come from while in some cases, some might have entered into the deporting countries using false passport bought illegally from criminal groups.

Language barriers and communication

Language barriers represent a significant challenge for non-African deportees upon their arrival in Africa. Many deportees hail from diverse linguistic backgrounds, often speaking languages that are not widely understood in their new environments. This lack of common language can lead to miscommunication, isolation, and difficulties in accessing essential services such as healthcare, legal aid, and employment opportunities. The emotional toll of feeling unheard and misunderstood can further exacerbate the already challenging transition they face after deportation.

The impact of language barriers extends beyond immediate communication difficulties; it can hinder the integration process into local communities. Deportees may struggle to build relationships and connect with locals, which is crucial for developing a support network. This social isolation can lead to feelings of loneliness and depression, compounding the mental health challenges many deportees experience. As they navigate a new culture, the inability to communicate effectively can leave them feeling alienated and vulnerable.

Legal challenges often arise due to language barriers, particularly when deportees are required to understand complex legal documents or court proceedings. The lack of interpreters or legal assistance in their native language can result in deportees being unable to advocate for their rights or understand the legal processes affecting their status. This situation may lead to unjust outcomes, as they may not fully comprehend the implications of their legal situations, further entrenching them in a cycle of disadvantage.

Community acceptance is also affected by language barriers. Locals may be hesitant to engage with individuals whose language they do not speak, leading to misconceptions and stereotypes. This social stigma can prevent deportees from finding employment or participating in community activities, reinforcing their marginalisation. Over time, these barriers can create a significant divide between deportees and the local population, hindering social cohesion and mutual understanding.

To address these challenges, the role of NGOs becomes crucial in facilitating language support and integration programmes. These organisations can provide language classes, cultural orientation, and resources that empower deportees to rebuild their lives. By bridging the communication gap, NGOs can help foster a sense of belonging and community acceptance, ultimately aiding in the mental health and well-being of deportees as they embark on their new journeys in Africa.

Building new social networks

The journey of non-African deportees to Africa often leads to the creation of new social networks that can significantly influence their integration into society. These networks are crucial for providing emotional support, access to resources, and a sense of belonging in a foreign environment. As deportees navigate their new realities, they often rely on connections formed with fellow deportees who share similar experiences, creating a community that fosters resilience and solidarity. The establishment of these networks can help alleviate feelings of isolation, which are common among those facing the stigma associated with deportation.

Building new social networks also involves engaging with local communities, which can be a double-edged sword for deportees. While some may find acceptance and understanding, others may face prejudice and societal rejection. The challenges of integrating into a new social fabric require deportees to be proactive, often seeking out organisations and support groups that can facilitate the process. These interactions are essential for overcoming the barriers of stigma and fostering a more inclusive environment for all immigrants.

The role of non-governmental organisations (NGOs) is particularly vital in this context. NGOs often act as intermediaries, helping deportees connect with local resources, legal assistance, and mental health support. By providing platforms for deportees to share their stories and experiences, these organisations help in the healing process and promote awareness among local populations. Furthermore, NGOs can also advocate for the rights of deportees, ensuring their voices are heard in discussions about immigration policies and human rights.

Cultural adjustment plays a significant role in the rebuilding of social networks for deported non-African immigrants. Many deportees face the challenge of reconciling their identities, as they may have spent significant parts of their lives in Western countries. This cultural dissonance can complicate relationships with both fellow deportees and local inhabitants. However, successful navigation of these cultural landscapes can lead to enriching exchanges and the formation of diverse networks that benefit all involved.

Ultimately, the journey of building new social networks is a critical component of the reintegration process for non-African deportees. It highlights the resilience of individuals who seek to create a new life despite the challenges they face. As these networks grow and evolve, they contribute not only to the personal development of deportees but also to the broader dialogue on immigration and social inclusion in African societies. The impact of these networks extends beyond individual experiences, reflecting the need for humane and supportive approaches to immigration policies worldwide.

Chapter 9: Influence of diaspora networks

The role of the diaspora in the reintegration of deported non-African immigrants is multifaceted and critical to their successful transition back into society. Many deportees arrive in their countries of origin with the hope of reconnecting with family and friends who may have settled abroad. This connection can play a vital role in their emotional and psychological well-being, as it provides a sense of belonging and support during a challenging time. The diaspora often serves as a bridge, facilitating the deportees' adaptation to their home country by sharing resources, information, and networks that can ease the reintegration process.

Diaspora networks have the potential to influence the socio-economic reintegration of deported individuals. Many deportees find themselves in precarious economic situations upon their return, often lacking the skills or resources needed to secure stable employment. However, diaspora connections can offer access to job opportunities, vocational training, and financial assistance. This support is crucial in helping deportees regain their independence and rebuild their lives, ultimately contributing to the overall economic health of their communities.

Moreover, the emotional support provided by diaspora communities can significantly impact the mental health of deported individuals. Facing the stigma of deportation can lead to feelings of isolation and depression among returnees. Having a supportive network from the diaspora can mitigate these effects, offering companionship and understanding. Such support systems are essential in helping deportees navigate the challenges of reintegration, as they can share coping strategies and experiences that resonate with those who have faced similar struggles.

The role of NGOs in supporting deported non-African immigrants is also intertwined with diaspora efforts. Many NGOs collaborate with diaspora groups to provide essential services. These partnerships enhance the resources available to deportees, ensuring they receive comprehensive support during their reintegration. The combined efforts of NGOs and diaspora networks create a more robust safety net for returnees, promoting successful integration and reducing the likelihood of recidivism.

In conclusion, the diaspora plays an indispensable role in the reintegration of deported non-African immigrants. Through emotional support, economic assistance, and collaboration with NGOs, diaspora networks can significantly ease the transition back into society for deportees. Their involvement not only aids individual deportees but also fosters a more inclusive and accepting environment within communities, ultimately benefiting society as a whole.

Economic Support from Diaspora Communities

Financial assistance from diaspora networks can alleviate some of these burdens, enabling deportees to establish themselves and contribute positively to their communities. By leveraging their international connections, diaspora members can facilitate access to job opportunities, business financing, and essential resources that are often scarce for returnees.

Many members of the diaspora are actively involved in mentoring and providing guidance to deported individuals, helping them navigate the complex landscape of employment and entrepreneurship in their home countries. This support can foster a sense of belonging and reduce the social stigma associated with deportation. By sharing their own experiences, diaspora members can inspire deportees to overcome the challenges they face, encouraging resilience and self-sufficiency.

Moreover, the economic impact of diaspora support can be significant for local economies. When deported individuals secure employment or start businesses with the help of their diaspora networks, they not only improve their own circumstances but also contribute to the economic development of their communities. This can create a ripple effect, leading to job creation and increased economic activity in areas that may have been struggling. As such, the interconnection between diaspora support and local economic revitalisation highlights the importance of these networks in the reintegration process.

However, the effectiveness of diaspora support is often influenced by the legal challenges faced by deported individuals. Many returnees encounter difficulties in obtaining necessary documentation, which can hinder their ability to access employment or start businesses. Diaspora communities can play a crucial role in advocating for policy changes that protect the rights of deportees and facilitate their reintegration. By raising awareness of these issues, diaspora members can help shift public perception and promote a more supportive environment for returnees.

In conclusion, the economic support from diaspora communities is essential for the successful reintegration of deported non-African immigrants to African countries. This support encompasses financial assistance, mentorship, and advocacy for legal rights, all of which contribute to the overall well-being of returnees. As these individuals navigate their new realities, the involvement of diaspora networks can significantly enhance their prospects, ultimately benefiting both the deportees and their communities at large.

Social and cultural contributions

The social and cultural contributions of non-African deportees to Africa are often overlooked amidst the complex narratives surrounding their deportation. These individuals bring with them unique perspectives, skills, and experiences that can enrich local communities. For instance, many deportees possess valuable professional skills in sectors such as technology, art, and education. Their diverse backgrounds can foster cultural exchange and innovation, bridging gaps between different communities and enhancing the social fabric of their new environments.

While some deportees may struggle with their identity and the perception of being an outsider, others actively work to establish new ties by engaging in local community initiatives. Their involvement can lead to greater acceptance and understanding, as they share their stories and contribute positively to their communities. This social interaction not only aids in their personal adjustment but also contributes to the broader dialogue on migration and integration.

Various organisations provide essential services such as legal assistance, mental health support, and vocational training to help them navigate the complexities of their new lives. By facilitating access to resources and fostering connections within local communities, these NGOs play a pivotal role in mitigating the challenges faced by deportees. Their efforts help empower individuals, enabling them to rebuild their lives and contribute to society.

Moreover, the cultural adjustment experiences of non-African deportees highlight the resilience and adaptability of these individuals. Many deportees must learn to navigate different cultural norms and practices while coping with the emotional fallout of deportation. Through community engagement, they often find a sense of belonging and purpose, which can significantly improve their mental health. This process of adjustment is not only crucial for the deportees themselves but also enriches the communities they join, creating a more diverse and inclusive environment.

Finally, the influence of diaspora networks can significantly aid in the reintegration process of deported individuals. These networks often provide crucial support systems, facilitating connections that can ease the transition into their new lives. By sharing resources, experiences, and opportunities, diaspora communities play a vital role in helping deportees navigate their challenges and achieve a sense of stability. This interconnectedness exemplifies the broader social and cultural contributions that non-African deportees can make, highlighting the importance of understanding and supporting their experiences in Africa.

Chapter 10: Overview of policies in key Western countries

The policies regarding deportation in key Western countries are shaped by a combination of national security concerns, immigration control, and international relations. Countries like the United States, the United Kingdom, and Australia have established frameworks that dictate the conditions under which immigrants can be deported. These policies often reflect a broader political climate that prioritises stringent immigration measures, which can lead to complex legal challenges for deportees upon arrival in their countries of origin, particularly in Africa.

In the United States, for instance, deportation policies have become increasingly harsh over the years, especially following the events of September 11, 2001. The focus has shifted towards the removal of individuals deemed a threat to national security, often resulting in the deportation of immigrants who may have lived in the country for many years. Similarly, the United Kingdom has implemented policies that allow for the removal of immigrants who have committed crimes, regardless of their ties to the community or family. This creates a legal quagmire for deportees, who may find themselves fighting against their deportation even after establishing lives in these countries.

The mental health impact of deportation on immigrants is significant and often overlooked in the discussions surrounding these policies. Deportees frequently experience trauma as they are uprooted from their communities, which can exacerbate pre-existing mental health issues or create new ones. The stigma attached to being deported also plays a crucial role in their mental well-being, as many returnees face social ostracism in their home countries. This stigma can hinder their ability to reintegrate and access support systems, further compounding their mental health struggles.

Social acceptance of deported individuals varies widely across different African nations, influenced by cultural perceptions of immigration and returnees. In some cases, deportees are welcomed back as individuals who have gained international experience, while in others, they are viewed with suspicion and disdain. This societal attitude can significantly affect their reintegration process and overall adjustment to life back in their home countries. The role of non-governmental organisations (NGOs) becomes vital in providing support, resources, and advocacy for these individuals, helping them navigate the challenges they face upon their deportation.

A comparative analysis of deportation policies across Western nations reveals stark differences in approach and implementation. Some countries have more humane systems that provide avenues for legal recourse, while others employ more draconian measures that leave deportees vulnerable to human rights violations. The experiences of specific nationalities among deported immigrants highlight the intersection of legal frameworks and individual narratives, showcasing the need for a more compassionate approach that considers the human impact of such policies. Understanding these dynamics is essential for fostering a supportive environment for deported immigrants as they seek to rebuild their lives in elsewhere.

The effectiveness of different approaches to managing the reintegration of non-African deportees into African societies varies greatly, influenced by both the policies implemented by Western countries and the local contexts in which deportees find themselves. For those shipped to their country of origin, many deportees arrive in their countries of origin with little support, facing immediate challenges such as socio-economic instability and cultural dislocation. The effectiveness of community-based support systems, including the role of non-governmental organisations (NGOs), has been crucial. These organisations often provide essential services and vocational training, which are vital for helping deportees navigate their new realities.

Legal challenges faced by most deportees can significantly hinder their reintegration. Many deportees find themselves in a precarious legal situation, lacking the necessary documentation to secure employment or access basic services. The effectiveness of legal advocacy varies, with some NGOs successfully negotiating with local governments to establish more inclusive policies, while others struggle against bureaucratic barriers. This disparity highlights the need for a more unified approach to legal support that can effectively address the unique circumstances of deported individuals from diverse backgrounds.

Deportees often grapple with trauma stemming from their deportation experience, exacerbated by the stigma associated with being an immigrant in their home countries. Effective mental health support, therefore, is essential for helping individuals rebuild their lives. Programs that incorporate culturally sensitive therapeutic practices have shown promise in mitigating the effects of trauma and aiding in the overall well-being of deportees, fostering a sense of belonging and acceptance within their communities.

When shipped to wrong countries, many face discrimination and prejudice, which can hinder their ability to connect with local communities and rebuild their lives. Initiatives aimed at raising awareness and promoting understanding of the deportation experience are vital for combating stigma. Community engagement activities that include deportees in cultural events can also enhance their acceptance and foster positive relationships within society, creating a more inclusive environment.

Overall, the comparative analysis of deportation policies across different Western countries reveals significant disparities in how deportees are treated upon their return. Countries with more supportive frameworks tend to experience better outcomes for their deportees, indicating that policy effectiveness is closely tied to the resources allocated for reintegration efforts. By learning from successful case studies and implementing best practices, both governments and NGOs can enhance the effectiveness of their approaches to support deportees, ultimately leading to more successful reintegration into society.

Lessons learned from policy comparisons

The examination of deportation policies across various Western countries reveals significant lessons that can inform future actions and reforms. Understanding the nuances of these policies highlights the diverse legal challenges faced by immigrants upon their deportation For instance, while some countries may have stringent regulations regarding deportation, others may adopt more lenient approaches, affecting the deportees' reintegration processes. This comparative analysis underscores the need for a more unified and humane approach to deportation, considering the human rights implications involved.

Another critical aspect highlighted through policy comparisons is the mental health impact experienced by deported immigrants. Many deportees arrive in their home countries with unresolved trauma stemming from their experiences in the host nations, exacerbated by the stigma they face upon return. The social stigma associated with deportation often leads to isolation and mental health struggles, indicating a pressing need for supportive interventions by local communities and NGOs. This recognition can pave the way for tailored mental health support systems that cater specifically to the needs of these individuals.

Additionally, the role of diaspora networks emerges as a pivotal factor in the reintegration of deported immigrants. In countries with strong diaspora connections, deportees often receive better support and resources that facilitate their adjustment back into society. The influence of these networks can also help combat the negative perceptions surrounding deportation, fostering a more accepting environment for returnees. This aspect of policy comparison illustrates the potential benefits of leveraging existing community structures to aid in the successful reintegration of deportees.

Case studies of specific nationalities among deported immigrants further enrich the understanding of these lessons. By examining the unique experiences of various groups, it becomes evident that cultural factors significantly influence the reintegration process. Each nationality brings its own set of challenges and resources, which highlights the necessity for tailored approaches in policy implementation and community support. This diversity within the deportee population calls for a more nuanced understanding of the individual and collective experiences of those affected by deportation.

Lastly, the analysis of the role of NGOs in supporting deported immigrants provides critical insights into how civil society can bridge the gap left by governmental policies. NGOs often play a vital role in offering legal assistance, mental health support, and community engagement opportunities that help deportees navigate their new circumstances. Their work not only aids in the immediate challenges faced by deportees but also fosters long-term social acceptance and integration, ultimately contributing to a more inclusive society. The lessons learned from these policy comparisons can thus inform more effective practices and advocacy strategies in the realm of deportation and immigrant support.

Chapter 11: Conclusion and future directions

Summary of key findings

This subchapter summarises the critical findings regarding the journey of deportees to new countries, highlighting the multifaceted challenges they face. Many deportees from Western countries encounter significant legal hurdles upon arrival, often struggling to navigate the complex legal systems in their host countries. These challenges can exacerbate feelings of isolation and dislocation, making reintegration into society particularly difficult for individuals who may already be vulnerable due to their deportation status.

Finally, a comparative analysis of deportation policies across different Western countries reveals varying approaches and their implications for deported individuals. Understanding these differences is crucial for advocating for more humane and just policies that consider the human rights of deportees. Overall, the findings emphasise the need for a comprehensive approach that addresses legal, mental health, social, and cultural aspects of the deportation experience for non-African immigrants sent to facilities in certain African countries.

Recommendations for policymakers

Policymakers must address the complexities surrounding the deportation of immigrants, considering the legal challenges they face upon their return. It is essential to develop frameworks that protect the rights of these individuals, ensuring that they are not subjected to arbitrary detention or discrimination. By establishing clear legal pathways for deportees, governments can facilitate a smoother reintegration process and reduce the likelihood of recidivism. This requires collaboration between legal experts, human rights organisations, and local authorities to create a comprehensive support system although this may be lacking in some countries.

The trauma experienced by deported immigrants often exacerbates existing mental health issues, leading to long-term psychological distress. Policymakers should invest in mental health resources and support services tailored specifically for deportees. This includes access to counselling and community support groups that can help individuals navigate their emotional challenges and rebuild their lives. By prioritising mental health, policymakers can significantly enhance the overall well-being of deported immigrants.

Social stigma surrounding deportation must also be addressed through public awareness campaigns that promote acceptance and understanding within local communities. Policymakers should collaborate with NGOs to create initiatives that foster positive narratives about deported individuals, highlighting their resilience and potential contributions to society. Education and outreach can play a pivotal role in dismantling harmful stereotypes, allowing deportees to reintegrate successfully and reduce feelings of isolation.

Policymakers should encourage the establishment of connections between deportees and their diaspora communities, which can provide vital support in terms of resources, mentorship, and job opportunities. By facilitating these networks, governments can empower deportees to leverage their existing connections, easing their transition back into society and helping them to rebuild their lives.

Lastly, a comparative analysis of deportation policies across different Western countries can offer valuable insights for policymakers in Africa. Understanding the varied approaches to deportation and reintegration can inform the development of more humane and effective policies. By learning from international best practices, African governments can enhance their strategies for addressing the challenges faced by non-African deportees, ensuring that human rights are upheld and that deportees receive the support they need to thrive in their new home countries if, of course they choose to live there.

Areas for further research

The subject of non-African deportees being shipped to detention camps in specific African countries offers a fertile ground for further research, particularly regarding the legal challenges faced by these individuals upon their arrival. Many deported immigrants encounter complex legal frameworks that often leave them vulnerable and without adequate protection. Examining the nuances of these legal challenges could illuminate the need for reforms in immigration policies and highlight the importance of ensuring that deportees are treated fairly under the law.

Another critical area for investigation is the mental health impact of deportation on non-African immigrants. The experience of being forcibly removed from one's home and returning to a country that may feel foreign can lead to significant psychological distress. Research into the mental health consequences, including anxiety, depression, and post-traumatic stress disorder, could provide essential insights into the support systems needed for these individuals as they navigate their reintegration into society.

Social stigma and community acceptance are also pivotal areas warranting further exploration. Deportees often face discrimination and social exclusion, which can hinder their ability to rebuild their lives. Understanding the dynamics of community acceptance and the factors that contribute to or alleviate stigma could guide interventions that foster more inclusive environments for returning immigrants.

Human rights implications of deportation policies in Western countries present another essential topic for research. The intersection of immigration enforcement and human rights continues to raise ethical questions about the treatment of deportees. Investigating these implications can help advocate for policy changes that uphold the dignity and rights of all individuals, regardless of their immigration status.

Finally, the role of NGOs in supporting deported non-African immigrants in Africa deserves closer examination. NGOs often play a crucial role in providing resources, legal aid, and emotional support to deportees. Researching the effectiveness of these initiatives and identifying best practices could enhance the support network available to those affected by deportation, ultimately aiding their reintegration and fostering a sense of belonging in their home countries. The following chapters are provided in order to address the different and peculiar nature of ALL deportees from united states being sent almost everywhere to countries that would accept these deportees, detainees and as Trump administration calls them, "illegal immigrants and criminals". The concluding chapters will cover the same theme of "Deported to the wrong country.

Chapter 12: Introduction to Trump's deportation Strategies

Immigration policies in the United States have long been a contentious issue, particularly during the Trump administration. The approach taken by President Trump marked a significant shift from previous practices, focusing heavily on deportation strategies that targeted undocumented immigrants and those seeking refuge. This subchapter will explore the various facets of these policies, including their historical context and the legal challenges they have faced, as well as the broader implications for the economy and society as a whole.

During Trump's presidency, the enforcement of immigration laws became more aggressive, resulting in a surge of deportation orders. This not only affected individuals but also had a profound impact on families and communities. Refugees found themselves in precarious positions, often facing uncertain futures as the administration sought to limit their entry into the country. The consequences of these strategies extended beyond the immediate effects on deported individuals, influencing public opinion and fuelling debates on human rights and the economy.

Legal challenges to deportation orders emerged as a significant aspect of Trump's immigration policies. Numerous lawsuits were filed, contesting the legality of the administration's actions and the potential violation of due process rights. These legal battles reflected the deep divisions within the country regarding immigration and highlighted the role of the judiciary in checking executive power. The outcomes of these cases not only shaped the enforcement of immigration laws but also raised questions about the balance between national security and humanitarian obligations.

Public opinion on immigration and deportation during Trump's presidency was notably polarised. Supporters of the administration argued that strict immigration policies were necessary for national security, while opponents viewed them as inhumane and detrimental to society. Advocacy and resistance movements gained momentum, with grassroots organisations rallying against deportation practices. These movements played a crucial role in raising awareness and mobilising communities to challenge the status quo and advocate for more humane immigration reform.

The role of state and local governments in Trump's deportation agenda also warrants attention. Many states took it upon themselves to counteract federal policies, implementing their own protections for undocumented immigrants. This pushback illustrated the complexities of immigration enforcement in a federal system, where local jurisdictions often grappled with the implications of federal policies on their communities. The economic consequences of these deportation strategies were profound, affecting labour markets and contributing to a climate of fear among immigrant populations, which in turn influenced broader economic stability.

Objectives of deportation strategies

The objectives of deportation strategies under Trump's administration were multifaceted, often reflecting a blend of political, economic, and social aims. Primarily, these strategies sought to fulfil a campaign promise to enforce stricter immigration controls, which resonated with a significant segment of the American populace that perceived immigration as a threat to job security and national identity. By emphasising enforcement, the administration aimed to project an image of strength and decisiveness, appealing to voters who valued a tough stance on immigration issues.

Economically, the administration's deportation strategies were justified by the argument that removing undocumented immigrants would free up jobs for American citizens and reduce the strain on public resources. However, this perspective overlooked the substantial contributions that immigrants make to the economy, particularly in sectors such as agriculture, construction, and services. The deportation of individuals who had established lives and businesses in the United States not only disrupted local economies but also raised concerns about the long-term impacts on economic growth and community stability.

Socially, these strategies were rooted in a narrative that framed immigrants as criminals or threats to public safety.

This rhetoric not only justified aggressive deportation practices but also fostered an atmosphere of fear among immigrant communities, leading to widespread anxiety about family separations and the potential for legal repercussions. The impact was profound, as many individuals faced the constant threat of deportation, which affected their mental health and overall sense of belonging in society.

Legal challenges to deportation orders became a significant objective for advocacy groups, who sought to protect the rights of individuals facing removal. These legal battles highlighted the complexities of immigration law and the often-arbitrary nature of deportation processes. As courts grappled with cases challenging the legality of deportation tactics, the outcomes influenced public opinion and shed light on the need for comprehensive immigration reform.

In summary, the objectives of deportation strategies during Trump's presidency were driven by a combination of political posturing, economic assumptions, and social narratives that ultimately shaped the landscape of immigration in the United States. The consequences of these strategies extended far beyond the immediate act of deportation, affecting families, communities, and the nation's economy as a whole. Understanding these objectives is crucial for evaluating the long-term implications of such policies and the ongoing debates surrounding immigration reform.

Chapter 13: Historical context of deportation practices in the USA

Early deportation policies

The early deportation policies implemented during Donald Trump's presidency marked a significant shift in the landscape of immigration enforcement in the United States. Prior to this period, while deportations were a reality, they were often conducted with a degree of discretion and prioritisation that aimed to focus on individuals with serious criminal backgrounds. Trump's aggressive approach, however, prioritised a broader range of undocumented immigrants, leading to a surge in deportations that affected families and communities across the nation.

One of the most notable aspects of these policies was the expansion of the categories of individuals targeted for deportation. Under the Trump administration, the enforcement priorities shifted to include not just those with criminal records, but also those who had committed minor infractions or had no criminal history at all. This change created an atmosphere of fear among immigrant communities, as individuals began to feel vulnerable to deportation regardless of their circumstances or contributions to society.

Legal challenges to these deportation orders emerged swiftly, as advocacy groups and affected individuals sought to contest the new measures. Courts were inundated with cases arguing that the policies violated due process rights and failed to consider the humanitarian aspects of individual cases. These legal battles highlighted the tension between the administration's hardline stance and the principles of justice and fairness that many believed should govern immigration enforcement.

Public opinion on immigration and deportation shifted during this time, with many Americans grappling with their views on the treatment of immigrants. Polls indicated a divided nation, with some supporting the tough measures as necessary for national security, while others condemned them as inhumane and counterproductive. This polarisation reflected broader societal debates about immigration, identity, and the values that should define the United States.

Historically, deportation practices have varied widely in the United States, influenced by economic conditions, political climates, and social attitudes. The early deportation policies of the Trump era can be seen as part of a long lineage of enforcement strategies that often-prioritised control over compassion. The economic consequences of these strategies were profound, affecting not only the individuals deported but also the communities left behind, which faced significant disruptions to their social and economic fabric.

The landscape of immigration policy in the United States has been profoundly shaped by key legislation and historical milestones. One of the pivotal moments was the Immigration and Nationality Act of 1965, which abolished the quota system based on nationality. This legislation marked a significant shift towards a more inclusive immigration policy, facilitating the entry of a diverse array of immigrants. However, the subsequent decades saw a series of legislative measures that increasingly restricted immigration, culminating in the controversial policies implemented during Donald Trump's presidency.

Under President Trump, the focus on deportation intensified, with the implementation of strategies such as the "zero tolerance" policy, which led to the separation of families at the border. This approach ignited fierce public debate and legal challenges, with numerous lawsuits filed against the administration's deportation orders. These legal battles highlighted the tension between federal immigration enforcement and the rights of individuals, revealing a complex web of legal precedents that shaped the outcomes of these cases.

Public opinion on immigration and deportation during Trump's tenure exhibited stark divisions. Polls indicated that while many Americans supported stricter immigration controls, a significant portion of the population expressed concern over the humanitarian implications of aggressive deportation strategies. Advocacy and resistance movements emerged in response to these policies, galvanising communities to fight against what they perceived as unjust deportation practices. Grassroots organisations played a crucial role in mobilising public sentiment and influencing policy discussions at local, state, and national levels.

The historical context of deportation practices in the United States reveals a longstanding pattern of fluctuating immigration policies, often influenced by economic conditions and political climates. Throughout American history, deportation has been used as a tool to manage population flows, with varying degrees of severity. The economic consequences of Trump's deportation strategies further complicate this narrative, as businesses and local economies faced repercussions from the loss of immigrant labour, which many industries rely on for their workforce.

As state and local governments navigated the complexities of Trump's deportation agenda, their responses varied significantly. Some jurisdictions embraced the administration's policies, while others resisted, enacting sanctuary laws to protect undocumented immigrants from deportation. This divergence underscores the critical role that local governance plays in shaping immigration enforcement, highlighting the ongoing debate over the balance of power between federal authority and local autonomy in immigration matters.

Changes in deportation practices over time

The evolution of deportation practices in the United States has been significantly shaped by political climates and public sentiment over the years. Historically, deportation was viewed as a necessary measure for maintaining law and order, often used sparingly and primarily against individuals who had committed crimes. However, the increase in immigration, particularly during the late 20th century, led to a more aggressive stance on deportation, culminating in policies that expanded the definition of deportable offences. The shift towards stricter deportation measures reflects broader societal attitudes towards immigrants, especially during periods of economic uncertainty.

Under Donald Trump's presidency, deportation practices underwent a dramatic transformation, with a marked increase in the number of individuals targeted for removal.

The administration's approach was characterised by a zero-tolerance policy that aimed to discourage illegal immigration through the threat of deportation. This strategy not only intensified existing practices but also introduced new methods, such as the use of local law enforcement to carry out immigration checks. The consequences of these policies were profound, affecting not only the individuals deported but also their families and communities.

The impact of Trump's immigration policies on refugees was particularly pronounced, as many asylum seekers found themselves subject to expedited deportation processes, often without adequate legal representation. Legal challenges emerged as a response to these harsh measures, with advocates arguing that such practices violated both domestic and international laws. Courts became battlegrounds for these issues, leading to a complex interplay between executive power and judicial oversight. The outcomes of these legal challenges often influenced public opinion and highlighted the contentious nature of immigration policy during this period.

Public opinion on immigration and deportation fluctuated throughout Trump's presidency, reflecting broader societal divisions. While some segments of the population supported the administration's hardline approach, viewing it as a necessary step for national security, others condemned it as inhumane and detrimental to the fabric of American society. Advocacy and resistance movements emerged in response, mobilising communities to fight against deportation orders and to support those affected. These movements played a crucial role in raising awareness and advocating for more humane immigration policies, often contrasting sharply with the government's stance.

The role of some state and local governments in Trump's deportation agenda played front and centre of the whole undertaking. Many states took it upon themselves to either comply with, resist, or navigate the complexities of federal immigration policies. Some local governments enacted measures to protect undocumented immigrants, while others collaborated with federal authorities to facilitate deportations. This divergence in responses highlights the intricate relationship between federal and local jurisdictions and underscores the ongoing debate over immigration enforcement in the United States. Ultimately, the changes in deportation practices over time reflect a broader narrative of societal attitudes, legal challenges, and the evolving landscape of immigration policy in America.

Chapter 14: Economic Consequences of Trump's deportation strategies

Impact on labour markets

The impact of Trump's deportation strategies on labour markets is multifaceted, revealing significant repercussions for both the economy and the workforce. As deportations increased, many industries that heavily relied on immigrant labour faced critical shortages. This was particularly evident in sectors such as agriculture, construction, and hospitality, where the sudden removal of workers led to disruptions in productivity and a rise in operational costs. Employers struggled to find domestic workers willing to fill these roles, which exacerbated the labour market's instability during this tumultuous period.

Moreover, the fear of deportation created an atmosphere of uncertainty among immigrant communities, which further affected labour participation rates. Many undocumented immigrants, who previously contributed significantly to the economy, chose to withdraw from the workforce or operate in the shadows to avoid detection. This withdrawal not only diminished the labour pool but also stunted economic growth, as businesses found it increasingly challenging to maintain their workforce in the face of aggressive deportation policies.

The economic consequences of these deportation strategies also manifested in broader societal implications. As industries struggled with labour shortages, the resulting decline in productivity often led to increased prices for consumers. Additionally, the loss of immigrant workers translated into reduced tax revenues for local and state governments, which rely on these contributions to fund essential services. This situation created a ripple effect, impacting not just the businesses directly involved but also the communities that depend on them.

In response to these challenges, advocacy and resistance movements emerged, calling attention to the economic ramifications of Trump's deportation agenda. These movements highlighted the indispensable role of immigrants in sustaining various sectors of the economy and urged for comprehensive immigration reform. Activists emphasised that a more humane approach to immigration would benefit not only those directly affected but also the economy as a whole, fostering a more inclusive and productive workforce.

Finally, the role of state and local governments cannot be overlooked in this discourse. Many localities sought to counteract the federal government's deportation policies by implementing sanctuary laws or providing support for immigrant workers. These initiatives aimed to protect vulnerable populations while also reinforcing the economic contributions of immigrants. The ongoing dialogue around immigration policy continues to evolve, underscoring the intricate relationship between deportation strategies and labour market dynamics, which remains a critical issue in contemporary economic discussions.

Effects on local economies

The deportation strategies implemented during Donald Trump's presidency have had profound impacts on local economies across the United States. As numerous immigrants faced the threat of removal, many chose to leave their jobs and communities, leading to significant labour shortages in various sectors. Industries such as agriculture, hospitality, and construction, which heavily rely on immigrant labour, experienced disruptions, affecting productivity and profitability. Consequently, local businesses struggled to maintain operations, resulting in a ripple effect that hindered economic growth in numerous communities.

Furthermore, the fear instilled by aggressive deportation policies led to a decrease in consumer spending. Immigrant families, uncertain about their future, often curtailed their expenditures, opting to save rather than spend on goods and services. This decline in consumer confidence had a detrimental effect on local businesses that depend on steady patronage to thrive. As spending diminished, the economic vitality of many regions waned, contributing to a slower recovery in areas already grappling with economic challenges.

Local governments also faced financial repercussions stemming from increased deportation activities. The costs associated with legal battles, public safety, and social services for affected families placed additional strain on municipal budgets. Many localities that once benefited from immigrant contributions to tax revenues now found themselves grappling with the fiscal fallout of decreased economic activity and increased social service demands. This situation has prompted some local governments to reconsider their stance on immigration, weighing the economic benefits of a diverse workforce against the challenges posed by federal deportation policies.

Moreover, community dynamics shifted as families were separated due to deportations, leading to long-term socio-economic impacts. The loss of residents not only reduced the workforce but also diminished the cultural fabric of communities. Schools faced declining enrolment numbers, impacting funding and resources, while local organisations that depend on volunteer support saw a decrease in participation. These changes have further exacerbated existing inequalities, making it increasingly difficult for communities to recover from the economic repercussions of these policies.

The advocacy and resistance movements that emerged in response to these deportation strategies highlighted the critical need for a more humane approach to immigration. Grassroots organisations and local leaders began to advocate for policies that recognise the contributions of immigrants to local economies and communities. As public opinion shifted, many began to see the value in supporting inclusive policies that not only protect vulnerable populations but also bolster economic resilience. The ongoing dialogue surrounding immigration and deportation continues to shape local economies, illustrating the complex interplay between policy and community well-being.

Long-term economic implications

The long-term economic implications of Donald Trump's deportation strategies are affecting numerous sectors across the United States. As the deportation of immigrants, particularly those in low-wage jobs, increases, industries reliant on this workforce, such as agriculture, construction, and hospitality, face acute labour shortages. These shortages can result in higher wages for remaining workers but may also lead to increased costs for consumers and a slowdown in economic growth. The ripple effects of these labour market disruptions can hinder the overall economy, affecting GDP growth and employment rates in the long run.

Moreover, the impact on communities that have historically been inhabited by immigrant populations cannot be overlooked. Many of these communities contribute significantly to local economies through consumer spending and entrepreneurship. When deportations occur, these communities may experience a decline in economic activity, leading to reduced revenue for local businesses and a corresponding decrease in tax revenues for state and local governments. This can strain public services and infrastructure, ultimately affecting the quality of life for all residents, regardless of their immigration status.

In addition to immediate economic disruptions, Trump's immigration policies may also deter future immigration. Potential immigrants often consider the political and economic climate of a country before relocating. If the United States is perceived as hostile towards immigrants, it may lose out on the benefits that come with a diverse workforce, including innovation and cultural enrichment. This loss could stymie the nation's ability to compete in a global economy that increasingly relies on skilled labour and diverse perspectives.

Legal challenges to deportation orders during Trump's presidency also have significant economic ramifications. Court battles and the uncertainty surrounding immigration status can create instability in the labour market, as workers may be hesitant to invest in long-term employment or housing. This hesitance can lead to a less dynamic economy, where businesses struggle to maintain a steady workforce. Furthermore, the costs associated with legal proceedings and the enforcement of deportation orders can divert resources away from other essential public services, compounding the economic impact.

Finally, public opinion on immigration and deportation under Trump plays a crucial role in shaping economic policies and outcomes. Advocacy and resistance movements against deportation have gained momentum, highlighting the economic contributions of immigrants. As these movements challenge the narrative surrounding immigration, they may influence policy changes that could mitigate some of the adverse economic effects of deportation strategies. In this context, the role of state and local governments becomes even more pivotal, as they navigate the tensions between federal immigration policies and the economic realities of their communities.

Chapter 15: Impact of Trump's immigration policies on refugees

Changes to asylum procedures

The changes to asylum procedures during Donald Trump's presidency marked a significant shift in the landscape of immigration policy in the United States. Under his administration, the criteria for granting asylum became increasingly stringent, reflecting a broader agenda aimed at reducing immigration. This included the implementation of the "Remain in Mexico" policy, which required asylum seekers to wait in Mexico while their claims were processed. Such measures not only delayed the processing of asylum applications but also exposed vulnerable individuals to dangerous conditions in border regions.

Legal challenges to these altered procedures arose swiftly, with various advocacy groups contesting the legitimacy of the new regulations. Courts were often tasked with determining the legality of policies that many argued undermined the right to seek asylum. These legal battles highlighted the tension between executive authority and judicial oversight in immigration matters. The outcomes of these cases not only affected individual asylum seekers but also set significant precedents for future immigration policy.

Public opinion on Trump's immigration policies revealed a nation divided. While some segments of the population supported stricter measures, viewing them as essential for national security, others condemned the changes as inhumane and a violation of international obligations to protect refugees. Advocacy and resistance movements emerged strongly during this period, rallying around the belief that the United States should uphold its long-standing commitment to providing refuge for those fleeing persecution.

The historical context of deportation practices in the United States provided a backdrop against which these changes were evaluated. Previous administrations had also enacted restrictive policies, but the scale and intensity of Trump's approach were unprecedented. This shift prompted discussions about the economic consequences of deportation, particularly concerning the contributions of immigrant communities to the workforce and local economies.

State and local governments played a crucial role in either supporting or resisting Trump's deportation agenda. Some states enacted laws to protect undocumented immigrants, while others collaborated with federal authorities to facilitate deportations. This duality underscored the complex dynamics at play in American immigration policy, reflecting broader societal debates about inclusion, human rights, and the economic implications of deportation strategies.

Consequences for refugee communities

The consequences of Donald Trump's deportation strategies have been particularly severe for refugee communities in the United States. Many individuals seeking asylum, fleeing persecution and violence in their home countries, found themselves facing increased scrutiny and hostility. The rapid implementation of strict immigration policies created an environment of fear, making it difficult for refugees to seek the protection they desperately needed. As a result, countless vulnerable individuals were deterred from pursuing their legal rights to asylum and safety.

International bodies have closely monitored and responded to the implications of Trump's deportation strategies. The United Nations High Commissioner for Refugees (UNHCR) has raised concerns regarding the potential violation of international refugee laws, particularly as many deported individuals may face persecution upon return to their home countries. This scrutiny highlights the tension between national immigration policies and global humanitarian obligations, prompting calls for a more compassionate approach towards refugees and asylum seekers.

In addition to the UNHCR, various humanitarian organisations have issued statements condemning the harsh nature of deportation practices. These bodies argue that such strategies not only endanger the lives of those being deported but also undermine the fundamental rights and dignity of individuals seeking a better life. The collective response from international entities underscores the need for the United States to re-evaluate its immigration stance and consider the broader implications of its policies on human rights and international relations.

Legal institutions around the world have also weighed in, with some foreign governments expressing their dissatisfaction with America's aggressive deportation tactics. This discontent has led to discussions about the potential for legal challenges that may arise from these practices, particularly in light of international law. Countries that advocate for human rights have urged the US to adhere to its commitments under various treaties, emphasising the importance of due process and protection for vulnerable populations.

Public opinion has played a significant role in shaping the responses from international bodies. As awareness of the economic and social consequences of Trump's deportation policies grows, many nations have called for more humane and fair immigration practices. This shift in public sentiment has prompted international organisations to advocate for reform, pushing for policies that prioritise human welfare over strict enforcement measures.

The historical context of deportation practices in the USA also informs the responses from international bodies. Past experiences with immigration policies reveal patterns of resistance and advocacy that continue to influence contemporary discussions. As the world watches the unfolding situation, it becomes increasingly clear that the consequences of Trump's deportation strategies extend beyond US borders, affecting global perceptions of immigration and human rights.

Chapter 16: Legal challenges to deportation orders during Trump's presidency

Overview of key legal cases

The legal landscape surrounding deportation during Donald Trump's presidency was marked by several key cases that highlighted the contentious nature of immigration policies. One notable case was the Supreme Court's decision in Department of Homeland Security v. Regents of the University of California, which addressed the legality of the DACA programme. This case underscored the tension between executive power and legislative intent, as the Court ultimately ruled that the Trump administration's attempt to rescind DACA was arbitrary and capricious, reflecting a significant legal pushback against deportation strategies.

Another pivotal case was the Ninth Circuit's ruling in East Bay Sanctuary Covenant v. Barr, which challenged the administration's policy that sought to restrict asylum eligibility for individuals who crossed the southern border illegally. The court's decision to block the enforcement of this policy illustrated the judiciary's role in checking executive authority, particularly in matters affecting vulnerable populations seeking refuge from violence and persecution.

In addition to these cases, the legal challenges to the so-called "public charge" rule also drew considerable attention. This rule aimed to deny green cards to immigrants who had used public benefits, and its implementation was met with multiple lawsuits. The courts' scrutiny of this policy revealed broader concerns about its potential economic consequences and the chilling effect it had on immigrant communities, ultimately leading to a stay on its enforcement.

Public opinion on these legal battles varied widely, reflecting deep divisions within American society regarding immigration. As court decisions emerged, advocacy and resistance movements gained momentum, mobilising citizens to stand against perceived injustices in deportation policies. These movements not only influenced public sentiment but also pressured state and local governments to adopt more humane stances on immigration enforcement, often in direct opposition to federal directives.

The historical context of deportation practices in the USA provides a crucial backdrop for understanding these legal cases. Past administrations have implemented various deportation strategies, but the aggressive tactics employed during Trump's presidency prompted renewed discussions about the economic and social implications of such policies. The interplay between legal challenges, public opinion, and advocacy efforts continues to shape the future of immigration law and policy in the United States.

Supreme court decisions

The Supreme Court has played a pivotal role in shaping the landscape of immigration policy during Donald Trump's presidency. Several landmark decisions have emerged in response to the administration's aggressive deportation strategies, highlighting the complex interplay between executive power and legal frameworks. Cases such as the challenge to the Deferred Action for Childhood Arrivals (DACA) programme illustrate not only the contentious nature of Trump's immigration policies but also the judiciary's role as a check on executive authority. These decisions have far-reaching implications for refugees and undocumented immigrants alike, as they navigate an increasingly hostile environment.

Legal challenges to deportation orders have surged during Trump's time in office, with many cases reaching the Supreme Court. The Court's rulings have often reflected a divided political landscape, with justices weighing the administration's immigration enforcement priorities against established legal protections for vulnerable populations. This judicial scrutiny has underscored the importance of legal representation for those facing deportation, as many have successfully argued for their rights in front of the highest court in the land. The outcomes of these cases have not only affected individual lives but have also set precedents for future immigration policies.

Public opinion on immigration and deportation has been deeply influenced by the Supreme Court's decisions. As rulings have emerged, they have sparked renewed debates among citizens, advocacy groups, and policymakers regarding the ethical implications of deportation practices. The Court's stances often reflect broader societal attitudes towards immigrants, revealing the complexities of public sentiment that can shift rapidly in response to legal developments. This dynamic illustrates the interplay between judicial action and public perception, shaping the narrative surrounding immigration in the United States.

The historical context of deportation practices in the USA adds another layer of complexity to the Supreme Court's decisions. Understanding past deportation trends and legal battles provides insight into how current policies have evolved. The Court's rulings often draw upon precedents from earlier cases, which can either reinforce or challenge long-standing practices. By examining the historical trajectory of deportation, one can appreciate the significance of the Supreme Court's role in influencing contemporary immigration discourse.

Finally, the economic consequences of Trump's deportation strategies have been a focal point in legal discussions. The Supreme Court's decisions have implications not only for individual immigrants but also for the broader economy. As businesses grapple with workforce shortages resulting from deportations, the Court's rulings can either exacerbate or alleviate these issues. Advocacy and resistance movements against deportation have also taken legal action, seeking to challenge the administration's policies in the courts. Thus, the Supreme Court remains a critical player in the ongoing dialogue surrounding immigration and economic stability in the United States.

Advocacy groups have played a crucial role in the legal challenges against deportation orders during Donald Trump's presidency. These organisations, often composed of legal experts, activists, and community members, mobilised a significant response to the administration's aggressive immigration policies. They sought to protect the rights of immigrants and refugees who faced the threat of removal from the United States. By utilising legal frameworks, advocacy groups aimed to challenge the constitutionality of deportation measures, drawing attention to the human impact of these policies.

The impact of Trump's immigration policies on refugees was particularly pronounced, as many advocacy groups focused on the plight of those fleeing violence and persecution. These organisations provided legal assistance, public education, and advocacy to ensure that vulnerable populations could access the protections afforded to them under international and domestic law. Their efforts highlighted the moral and humanitarian implications of deportation, framing these legal challenges as not merely political but as essential to preserving human dignity and rights.

In addition to legal assistance, advocacy groups also played a significant role in shaping public opinion on immigration and deportation. They engaged in campaigns to raise awareness about the realities of deportation, presenting personal stories of those affected to foster empathy and understanding. By humanising the issue, these groups sought to shift the narrative surrounding immigration, challenging the often-negative portrayals in mainstream media and political discourse.

Moreover, the historical context of deportation practices in the USA provided a backdrop for the advocacy efforts during Trump's presidency. Groups drew parallels between current policies and past injustices, emphasising that the struggle for immigrant rights has deep roots in American history. This historical perspective not only informed their legal strategies but also helped to mobilise broader coalitions of support, including from those who may not have previously engaged with immigration issues.

Ultimately, the role of advocacy groups in legal challenges against deportation orders serves as a testament to the power of collective action. Their resilience and commitment to justice have not only influenced legal outcomes but have also inspired a movement that continues to resist and challenge the deportation agenda. As these groups navigate the complexities of the legal system and public sentiment, their efforts underscore the ongoing struggle for immigrant rights and the importance of advocacy in the face of systemic challenges.

Chapter 17: Public Opinion on Deportation under Trump

Polling data regarding immigration and deportation strategies under Donald Trump's administration reveals a complex landscape of public sentiment. Many surveys conducted during his presidency indicated a stark divide among Americans concerning the treatment of undocumented immigrants. While a significant portion of the population supported stricter immigration enforcement, there was also a notable faction advocating for more humane policies towards refugees and those seeking asylum. This duality reflects the broader tensions within American society regarding national identity and humanitarian responsibility.

Trends in polling data show fluctuations in public opinion as Trump's deportation policies evolved. Initially, his hardline stance garnered substantial support, particularly among his base, which viewed immigration as a threat to jobs and security. However, as stories of family separations and the impact on communities surfaced in the media, public support began to wane. This shift illustrates how the human aspect of deportation policies can influence public perception and political discourse, often leading to calls for reform.

Legal challenges to deportation orders during Trump's presidency also played a significant role in shaping public opinion. Several high-profile court cases brought attention to the potential overreach of executive power in immigration enforcement. These legal battles not only impacted the lives of those directly involved but also sparked broader discussions about the legitimacy and morality of the administration's strategies. Polling data reflected increased awareness and concern regarding the implications of these legal decisions on immigrant rights and due process.

The historical context of deportation practices in the USA further informs current public attitudes towards Trump's policies. While deportation has long been a tool of immigration control, the scale and intensity of recent strategies marked a departure from previous practices. Polling trends reveal that many Americans are increasingly aware of this historical trajectory, leading to greater scrutiny and debate about the fairness of current policies. This historical awareness has prompted advocacy and resistance movements that challenge the status quo and seek to protect vulnerable populations.

Lastly, the role of state and local governments in Trump's deportation agenda has been pivotal in shaping public opinion. Many jurisdictions have opted to resist federal directives, reflecting a growing movement towards sanctuary policies aimed at protecting undocumented immigrants. Polling data indicates that such local actions resonate with a considerable segment of the population, highlighting a desire for more compassionate approaches to immigration. Overall, the interplay of polling data and public sentiment illustrates the evolving landscape of immigration policy in the United States, marked by both division and calls for change.

The media representation of immigration issues under Donald Trump's administration has played a crucial role in shaping public perception and policy. News outlets have often focused on the dramatic narratives surrounding deportations, presenting stories that evoke strong emotional responses. This has led to a polarised view of immigrants, where they are frequently depicted as either threats to national security or victims of an oppressive regime. The emphasis on sensational stories can overshadow the complexities of immigration policies and their economic implications.

Influence of public opinion on policy

Public opinion has played a pivotal role in shaping immigration policy in the United States, particularly during Donald Trump's presidency. The attitudes and beliefs of citizens regarding immigrants and deportation have been influenced by a myriad of factors, including economic concerns, national security, and social narratives. As Trump pursued aggressive deportation strategies, public sentiment fluctuated, often reflecting deeper societal divisions over the issue. This dynamic relationship between public opinion and policy highlights how political leaders respond to the electorate while also attempting to guide public perceptions through rhetoric and actions.

The impact of Trump's immigration policies on refugees further illustrates the significance of public opinion. Many Americans expressed empathy towards vulnerable populations seeking asylum, while others viewed such immigration as a threat to national security. The contrasting views led to heated debates across media platforms, with advocacy groups mobilising support for refugees and challenging deportation orders. This public discourse not only influenced the actions of lawmakers but also prompted various legal challenges that arose in response to the policies implemented by the Trump administration.

Legal challenges to deportation orders during Trump's presidency were often propelled by shifts in public opinion. As communities reacted to high-profile deportation cases, legal advocates seized the moment to contest the administration's practices in courts. Public outrage over perceived injustices served to galvanise support for legal interventions, illustrating how grassroots movements can reshape judicial outcomes. The courts became a battleground where public sentiment was reflected, as judges occasionally cited the potential harm to families and communities in their rulings against deportations.

Historically, the context of deportation practices in the USA reveals a continuous interplay between public opinion and policy. Previous administrations have faced similar challenges, yet the rhetoric surrounding Trump's approach was markedly different. His portrayal of immigrants as criminals resonated with certain segments of the population, further polarising the debate. This historical perspective allows for a better understanding of how current attitudes have evolved and how they may continue to influence future immigration policies.

The economic consequences of Trump's deportation strategies have also been a focal point of public discourse. Many argued that deportation not only harmed families but also had broader implications for local economies reliant on immigrant labour. Advocacy and resistance movements emerged, pushing back against the narrative of immigrants as economic burdens. State and local governments found themselves caught in the crossfire, as they navigated the complexities of enforcing federal immigration laws while responding to the concerns of their constituents. This multifaceted situation underscores the critical role that public opinion plays in shaping immigration policy and the political landscape at large.

Chapter 18: Advocacy and resistance against deportation

Grassroots organising and activism have emerged as powerful responses to the deportation strategies employed during Trump's presidency. These movements are often spearheaded by local communities that are directly affected by immigration policies. Individuals and organisations band together to amplify their voices, advocating for the rights of immigrants and challenging the systemic injustices that have arisen from strict deportation efforts. In this climate of fear and uncertainty, grassroots activism plays a crucial role in mobilising support and fostering solidarity among diverse groups.

The impact of Trump's immigration policies on refugees and undocumented immigrants has galvanised many to take action. Advocacy groups have sprung up across the nation, using various methods such as protests, social media campaigns, and community outreach to highlight the human cost of deportation. They seek to educate the public on the complexities of immigration and the need for compassionate policies that respect human rights. As these movements gain traction, they challenge not only the policies themselves but also the narratives surrounding immigration and deportation.

Legal challenges to deportation orders have also become a focal point for grassroots organisations. These groups often collaborate with legal experts to provide resources and assistance to those facing deportation. By raising awareness about the legal options available, they empower individuals to fight back against unjust deportation orders. The intersection of grassroots activism and legal advocacy illustrates the multifaceted approach needed to combat the harsh realities imposed by Trump's immigration strategies.

Public opinion on immigration and deportation has been influenced significantly by grassroots efforts. Through storytelling and personal testimonies, activists have humanised the issue, shifted perceptions and encouraged empathy towards those affected. This has led to increased public support for reforming immigration policies and resisting deportation practices. As more individuals recognise the complexities of the situation, there is a growing demand for change that reflects the values of justice and equality.

The role of state and local governments in Trump's deportation agenda cannot be underestimated. Grassroots organisations often engage with these entities to advocate for policies that protect immigrant communities. By lobbying local officials and participating in town hall meetings, activists work to hold governments accountable for their actions. This grassroots pressure can lead to significant policy shifts at the local level, demonstrating the power of collective action in the face of federal deportation strategies.

Role of non-profit organisations

The role of non-profit organisations in the context of Trump's deportation strategies has been pivotal in providing support, advocacy, and legal assistance to affected communities. These organisations have stepped in to fill the gaps left by governmental agencies, offering vital resources to immigrants facing the threat of deportation. Non-profits have mobilised quickly to respond to the increased fears and uncertainties that arose during Trump's presidency, particularly in light of aggressive immigration enforcement policies.

Non-profits have not only provided immediate assistance, such as food, shelter, and legal representation but have also engaged in broader advocacy efforts. They have worked tirelessly to raise public awareness about the consequences of deportation on families and communities. By sharing personal stories and statistics, these organisations have sought to humanise the issue, encouraging a more compassionate public response and challenging the prevailing narratives surrounding immigration.

Legal challenges to deportation orders have also been a significant focus for many non-profit organisations. They have provided crucial legal support to individuals facing deportation, helping to navigate the complexities of immigration law. This legal advocacy has often involved collaboration with pro bono lawyers and law firms, aiming to contest unjust deportation orders and protect the rights of immigrants.

Moreover, non-profits have played a vital role in fostering community resilience and solidarity. They have organised grassroots movements and campaigns, encouraging local communities to stand up against deportation practices. This mobilisation has been essential in galvanising public opinion and influencing policy discussions at both local and national levels, highlighting the importance of community engagement in the fight against unjust immigration policies.

In summary, non-profit organisations have emerged as critical players in the landscape of immigration and deportation during Trump's presidency. Their multifaceted contributions, from legal representation to community advocacy, have not only provided essential support to individuals but have also shaped the broader discourse on immigration. As the situation continues to evolve, the role of these organisations remains vital in advocating for immigrant rights and challenging harmful policies.

Case studies of successful resistance

Throughout history, resistance against unjust deportation practices has emerged from various communities, showcasing the resilience and determination of those affected. During Trump's presidency, numerous grassroots movements took shape, mobilising individuals and organisations to stand against the administration's aggressive immigration policies. These movements often highlighted personal stories of families torn apart and the economic repercussions of deportation on local communities, galvanising public support and fostering solidarity among diverse groups.

One notable case study is that of the "Sanctuary Cities," where local governments adopted policies to protect undocumented immigrants from deportation. Cities like San Francisco and New York implemented these policies, refusing to cooperate with federal immigration enforcement. Their bold stance not only provided a safe haven for immigrants but also sparked a national debate regarding states' rights and the federal government's role in immigration enforcement, effectively shifting public opinion in favour of immigrant protection.

Legal challenges also played a significant role in resisting deportation orders during this period. Advocacy groups, such as the American Civil Liberties Union (ACLU), filed lawsuits against the Trump administration, arguing that many deportation practices violated constitutional rights. These legal battles underscored the importance of the judiciary in providing a check on executive power, and in several instances, courts ruled in favour of immigrants, temporarily halting deportations and providing a reprieve for many families.

Moreover, public opinion on immigration and deportation shifted significantly during Trump's tenure, largely due to the relentless advocacy efforts by grassroots organisations. Campaigns that humanised immigrants through storytelling and public outreach helped to challenge the negative narratives propagated by the administration. This shift was evident in various polls, where a growing percentage of Americans began to support pathways to citizenship and opposed harsh deportation measures, reflecting a changing societal perspective on immigration.

In summary, the resistance against Trump's deportation strategies found expression through various means, including local government initiatives, legal challenges, and shifts in public opinion. These case studies not only illustrate the power of advocacy and community solidarity but also highlight the ongoing struggles faced by immigrants and their allies in the fight for justice. As these movements continue to evolve, they remind us of the importance of standing against policies that threaten human dignity and economic stability.

Chapter 19: Role of state and local governments in Trump's deportation agenda

The cooperation between state and local authorities with federal immigration agencies has been a contentious issue during Trump's presidency. Local police departments and state governments were often faced with the dilemma of whether to align themselves with federal deportation strategies or to uphold the trust of their communities. This collaboration sometimes took the form of agreements like 287(g), which allowed local law enforcement to act as immigration agents. Such partnerships raised significant concerns about racial profiling and community safety, as many felt that they undermined the relationship between immigrant communities and law enforcement.

Federal authorities, particularly ICE (Immigration and Customs Enforcement), sought to strengthen their operations by relying on local resources. This strategy was presented as necessary for national security and public safety, yet it often resulted in the increased targeting of vulnerable populations. Immigrant advocates argued that these practices led to fear and distrust within communities, making individuals less likely to report crimes or cooperate with police. The chilling effect of these policies highlighted the complex interplay between federal enforcement and local governance.

The legal challenges to deportation orders during Trump's presidency often included arguments against the legitimacy of these cooperative agreements. Courts were asked to consider whether local authorities had the legal mandate to enforce federal immigration laws. Some rulings suggested that such collaborations could violate constitutional protections against unreasonable searches and seizures. This legal landscape added another layer of complexity to the already fraught relationship between federal and local governments regarding immigration enforcement.

Public opinion on immigration and deportation under Trump was deeply divided, with many Americans supporting strict enforcement while others advocated for more humane treatment of immigrants. This dichotomy was reflected in the actions of local governments, some of which chose to resist federal directives in favour of protecting their residents. Advocacy and resistance movements emerged, pushing back against deportation tactics and calling for sanctuary policies that would limit local cooperation with federal authorities.

Historically, deportation practices in the USA have undergone significant evolution, influenced by shifting political landscapes. The current era under Trump represents a stark departure from earlier policies that often focused on integration rather than removal. Understanding this historical context is vital for comprehending the economic consequences of these deportation strategies. The impact on local economies, particularly in areas with large immigrant populations, underscores the importance of cooperation—or lack thereof—between federal and local authorities in shaping the future of immigration policy in the United States.

Sanctuary cities have become a significant focal point in the debate surrounding immigration policy in the United States, particularly during and after the Trump presidency. These municipalities have adopted policies that limit cooperation with federal immigration enforcement, aiming to protect undocumented immigrants from deportation. The emergence of sanctuary cities has sparked a variety of legislative responses at both federal and state levels, with proponents arguing for the protection of vulnerable populations and opponents claiming that such policies undermine national security and the rule of law.

In response to the rise of sanctuary cities, the Trump administration implemented various measures to penalise these localities. This included threats to withhold federal funding from jurisdictions that did not comply with federal immigration laws. These actions prompted legal challenges from several sanctuary cities, which argued that the federal government was overstepping its boundaries by coercing local governments into enforcing immigration laws. The courts have been involved in interpreting the balance of power between federal and state authorities, leading to ongoing legal battles that continue to shape the landscape of immigration enforcement.

Public opinion regarding sanctuary cities is deeply divided, reflecting broader sentiments towards immigration and deportation policies during Trump's presidency. Supporters of sanctuary cities argue that they foster community safety and trust between immigrants and local law enforcement, allowing individuals to report crimes without fear of deportation. Conversely, critics maintain that these policies contribute to increased crime and hinder law enforcement efforts. This dichotomy illustrates the complexities of public sentiment on immigration, revealing how perceptions can be influenced by political rhetoric and media coverage.

Historically, the concept of sanctuary is not new; it has roots in various social movements and religious practices aimed at protecting individuals from persecution. However, the contemporary application of sanctuary cities has taken on a unique role in the context of Trump's deportation strategies. The response of state and local governments illustrates a broader resistance movement against federal immigration policies, highlighting the tensions between local autonomy and federal authority. This historical context is essential for understanding the current legislative landscape and the motivations behind sanctuary city policies.

The economic consequences of Trump's deportation strategies are also significant, affecting both local economies and the broader national landscape. Sanctuary cities often argue that their policies contribute to economic stability by allowing immigrant communities to thrive without the constant threat of deportation. As these cities navigate the challenges posed by federal immigration enforcement, they also face economic pressures that require careful balancing of resources. Ultimately, the interplay between sanctuary cities and legislative responses will continue to evolve, reflecting the ongoing struggle over immigration policy in the United States.

The impact of local policies on deportation

The impact of local policies on deportation during Trump's presidency has been profound, as state and local governments took varied approaches to immigration enforcement. Some jurisdictions embraced the administration's hardline stance, actively cooperating with federal authorities to identify and detain undocumented immigrants. This cooperation often stemmed from a belief that stricter enforcement would lead to safer communities, reflecting a perception that immigrants were linked to crime and social instability. However, this alignment with federal policies also sparked significant backlash from local communities and advocacy groups, who argued that such measures were not only inhumane but also counterproductive to public safety.

Chapter 20: Conclusion and future implications

The economic fallout from Donald Trump's deportation strategies has revealed significant consequences for various sectors in the United States. The focus on mass deportations has not only affected the lives of countless undocumented immigrants but has also strained local economies reliant on immigrant labour. As businesses grapple with workforce shortages, the ripple effects are felt across communities that depend on these essential workers for both economic stability and growth.

Public opinion on immigration and deportation under Trump's presidency showcased a divided nation. While some segments of the population supported aggressive deportation measures as a means to enhance national security, others raised concerns about the humanitarian implications and the impact on families. This dichotomy highlights the complexities surrounding immigration policy in the United States, where perspectives are often influenced by economic realities and personal experiences.

Legal challenges to deportation orders during Trump's tenure underscored the contentious nature of his immigration policies. Numerous lawsuits were filed by advocacy groups aiming to protect the rights of immigrants and challenge the constitutionality of these orders. The judiciary's role became a critical battleground, reflecting the broader societal debate over immigration enforcement and the limits of executive power.

In historical context, the deportation practices under Trump's administration can be seen as part of a long-standing tradition of immigration control in the United States. However, the scale and intensity of these strategies marked a departure from previous practices, prompting a resurgence of advocacy and resistance movements. These grassroots organisations emerged to support affected individuals and families, highlighting the moral imperative to address the injustices stemming from harsh deportation policies.

State and local governments played a crucial role in shaping the implementation of Trump's deportation agenda. Many jurisdictions resisted federal mandates, choosing to adopt more humanitarian approaches to immigration enforcement. This tension between state and federal authorities illustrated the complexities of governance in the realm of immigration, revealing a landscape where local leaders sought to prioritise community cohesion over divisive federal policies.

Considerations for future immigration policy

As the United States grapples with the implications of former President Trump's deportation strategies, it becomes increasingly important to consider the future of immigration policy. The harsh realities faced by immigrants under these policies have sparked significant debate about the direction immigration laws should take moving forward. Policymakers must reflect on the economic, social, and humanitarian aspects of immigration, ensuring that future policies are both effective and just, while recognising the contributions that immigrants make to society.

One crucial consideration is the economic impact of deportation policies on both local and national economies. The abrupt removal of immigrants, who often play integral roles in various industries, can lead to labour shortages and disrupt economic stability. Future immigration policies should aim to create pathways for legal residency that support economic growth, recognising the essential roles that immigrants fill in the workforce and the overall economy.

Many individuals seeking refuge in the United States are fleeing violence, persecution, or dire economic circumstances. As policymakers contemplate new strategies, they must prioritise the protection of vulnerable populations and ensure that immigration policies reflect a commitment to human rights. This involves re-evaluating the criteria for refugee status and providing adequate support for those in need.

Public opinion plays a significant role in shaping immigration policy. The divisive nature of Trump's deportation agenda has highlighted stark contrasts in how different segments of the population view immigration. Future policies should take into account the evolving attitudes of the public, fostering a dialogue that emphasises empathy and understanding rather than fear and division. Engaging communities in discussions about immigration can lead to more inclusive policies that reflect the values of American society.

Finally, the role of state and local governments in immigration enforcement must be clearly defined in future policies. The decentralisation of immigration authority has led to varied practices across the country, often resulting in a patchwork of enforcement strategies. Establishing a cohesive national framework that clarifies the responsibilities of state and local governments can help ensure that policies are implemented fairly and consistently, ultimately contributing to a more stable and humane immigration system.

Legacy of Trump's deportation strategies

The legacy of Trump's deportation strategies is one that has left an indelible mark on the United States' immigration landscape. During his presidency, Trump implemented aggressive policies aimed at deterring illegal immigration, which included the controversial family separation policy and the expansion of deportation powers. These strategies not only affected millions of undocumented immigrants but also reshaped public discourse around immigration, creating a climate of fear and uncertainty among immigrant communities.

The impact of these policies was particularly pronounced on refugees seeking asylum. Many faced heightened scrutiny and obstacles in their pursuit of safety, as Trump's administration sought to limit the number of accepted asylum seekers. Legal challenges emerged in response to these policies, highlighting the tensions between executive authority and judicial oversight. Courts were often called upon to adjudicate the legality of deportation orders and the administration's adherence to international human rights standards.

Public opinion on immigration during Trump's presidency was sharply divided. Supporters of his policies viewed them as necessary for national security and economic stability, while opponents condemned them as inhumane and a violation of fundamental rights. This polarization was reflected in the activism and advocacy movements that arose in response to the administration's actions, as community organisations rallied to protect the rights of immigrants and challenge the legitimacy of deportations.

The historical context of deportation practices in the United States reveals that Trump's strategies were not entirely unprecedented, yet they marked a significant escalation in enforcement and rhetoric. Previous administrations had also pursued deportation, but Trump's approach was characterised by a more confrontational stance that sought to criminalise undocumented immigration. This shift has prompted discussions about the long-term economic consequences of such policies, particularly concerning the labour market and the contributions of immigrant communities to the economy.

State and local governments played a crucial role in the implementation of Trump's deportation agenda. Some jurisdictions embraced the federal government's stance, while others resisted by enacting sanctuary policies to protect immigrants from deportation. This divergence in responses has highlighted the complexities of immigration enforcement in a federal system and the ongoing battle over the direction of immigration policy in the United States. The legacy of Trump's deportation strategies will likely continue to influence immigration debates for years to come.

Also, by DM Ole Kiminta

How the Western Democracies failed the world (KBros)
Supporting Refugees in their Homelands (Kbros)
Dissuading Global War Mongers (KBros)
Dissuading war mongers (KBros)
La Libération Monétaire en Afrique (KBros)
Canada Post: Management failure to modernise mail systems
Live to be 200 (KBros)
Aim to live to be 200 (KBros)
Western democracies failed the world economies (KBros)
Wrong foot forward: US-Canada trade wars (KBros)
Canada begs to differ: Never a 51st state of USA (KBros)
Tethered to the Kitchen (KBros)
Nous ne pouvons pas être le 51e État des États-Unis (KBros)
Nous ne serons jamais le 51ème état des États-Unis. (KBros)
The Nephilim and the erosion of moral boundaries (KBros)
Every human is an advocate for World Peace (KBros)
The diplomatic dilemma of Western Sahara (KBros)
Every human: Advocate for World Peace (KBros)
The last blue planet (KBros)
Europeans divided & shaped Arab World (KBros)
Thuggery: What led to October 7th incident? (Kbros)
Breaking Free: Abandoning dependency on foreign currencies in Africa (Kindle Edition)
When white people were slaves: White Slavery (Kindle Edition)
Les consequences des colons francais sur Amazighs marocains: Contexte historique de la colonisation francais au Maroc (French Edition) Kindle Edition
L'Écoute qui Transforme: Renforcer la Confiance des Enfants à l'École: L'importance de la communication enfants-enseignants en classe (French Edition) Kindle Edition
Mastering Emotions: How to avoid Anger and jealousy: Anger and jealousy are destructive (Kindle Edition)
Maasai initiation in today's society (Kindle edition)
Hidden dangers of fully integrated AI world: Quality education with AI for future generation (Kindle edition)
One Africa: The premise & perils of political integration (Kindle)
Early foreign visitors into African nations: Fortune seekers (Kindle)
Deported to the wrong country: Impact of Trump's deportations

References

1) Current affairs in social media
2) Trump administration on news media
3) Local and foreign documentaries on deportations
4) Local and foreign news media (immigration)
5) American past administrations on immigration
6) Trump's previous administration policies
7) Regular white house briefings on journalists
8) American history (text books on political history)